A NOTE TO THE READER:

To better serve you, I've created discussion questions for
The Fruitful Wife that you can use for group studies and
individual reflection. These free resources can be found at:

www.hungryplanet.net/downloads

Sincerely,

Hayley DiMarco

Other Crossway Books by Hayley DiMarco:

Die Young: Burying Your Self in Christ,
Hayley DiMarco and Michael DiMarco (2011)

love joy peace patience kindness goodness faithfulness gentleness and self-control

CULTIVATING A LOVE ONLY GOD CAN PRODUCE

the Fruitful Wife

Hayley DiMarco

::: CROSSWAY

WHEATON, ILLINOIS

Published in association with ChristopherFerebee.com, Attorney and Literary Agent.

Cover design and image: Connie Gabbert

Interior design and typesetting: Kevin Lipp

First printing 2012

Printed in the United States of America

Unless otherwise indicated, Scripture quotations are from the ESV® Bible (*The Holy Bible, English Standard Version®*), copyright © 2001 by Crossway. Used by permission. All rights reserved.

GOD'S WORD is a copyrighted work of God's Word to the Nations Bible Society. Quotations marked GOD'S WORD are used by permission. Copyright 1995 by God's Word to the Nations Bible Society. All rights reserved.

Scripture references marked NIV are taken from The Holy Bible, New International Version®, NIV®. Copyright © 1973, 1978, 1984 by Biblica, Inc.™ Used by permission. All rights reserved worldwide.

Scripture references marked NKJV are from *The New King James Version*. Copyright © 1982, Thomas Nelson, Inc. Used by permission.

Emphases in Scripture quotations have been added by the author.

Trade paperback ISBN: 978-1-4335-3070-8
PDF ISBN: 978-1-4335-3071-5
Mobipocket ISBN: 978-1-4335-3072-2
ePub ISBN: 978-1-4335-3073-9

Library of Congress Cataloging-in-Publication Data

DiMarco, Hayley.
    The fruitful wife : cultivating a love only God can produce
/ Hayley DiMarco.
      p. cm.
Includes bibliographical references.
    ISBN 978-1-4335-3070-8
    1. Wives—Religious life. 2. Christian women—Religious
life. 3. Fruit of the Spirit. I. Title.
BV4528.15.D56   2012
248.8'435—dc23   2012013408

Crossway is a publishing ministry of Good News Publishers.

VP   22   21   20   19   18   17   16   15
15   14   13   12   11   10   9   8   7   6   5   4   3   2

CONTENTS

PROLOGUE

The Fruitful Wife isn't a book about making your life more amazing, though it certainly can do that. *The Fruitful Wife* is about experiencing a life filled with the fruit, or produce, of God the Holy Spirit. It's not about the perfect woman, because it's not written by the perfect woman, but it's about a life set on looking away from yourself so that you can better concentrate on the Father. So *The Fruitful Wife* is about what happens in the life of a woman who understands the effect of having the all-knowing, all-powerful, all-loving, perfect, and holy God of the universe take up residence in her body. *The Fruitful Wife* is about having something to show for your years on this earth. It's about producing rather than destroying, and it's about giving as well as getting. James MacDonald once said that if God isn't changing you, then he hasn't saved you. And this is my firm belief. A life filled with the life of God is one that is ever changing, ever pruning, ever growing, and ever flourishing.

There have been times in my life when I have been fruitful and times when I've struggled and been barren and unproductive. So this work isn't about my perfect life or my perfect devotion but about our perfect God and his unceasing grace and forgiveness for our less than fruitful attempts to live lives filled with the fruit of the Spirit. I hope that as you take this journey with me you'll be encouraged by the reminders found in these pages of the goodness of God and his power to bring all that goodness to fruition in your own life.

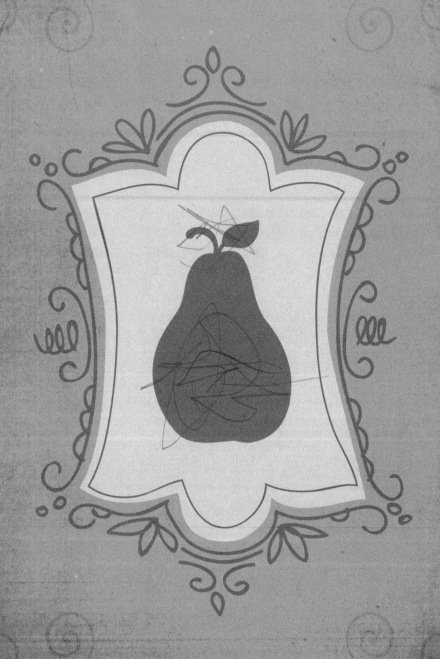

INTRODUCTION

INTRODUCTION

What Have We Done?

You will recognize them by their fruits.

—MATTHEW 7:20

The fruit of the Spirit is love, joy, peace, patience, kindness, goodness, faithfulness, gentleness, self-control.

—GALATIANS 5:22–23

The fruit of my first year of marriage was a lot of broken plates. In that year I produced more broken plates and angry screams than probably anything else. If the fruit of the Spirit in you is love, joy, peace, patience, kindness, goodness, faithfulness, gentleness, and self-control, I was a barren tree (that liked to throw plates).

While we were dating, I was a fruitful woman. I was in love, joyful, peaceful. I was patient with God because God had finally brought my Mr. Perfect, though I was a little impatient about tying the knot; the old clock was ticking, after all. But I wasn't struggling with impatience like I did before I met Michael. As for kindness, that was easy. I wanted to please him. He was certainly pleasing me, and so being kind in return was effortless. I was just overflowing fruit in my life. And then it all changed.

See, Michael and I got married later in life than many couples. We were both in our thirties when we eloped to the Bahamas. You might say that by your third decade on earth, you are set in your ways, used to life on your own, and you'd be right. So when we moved in together, our worlds turned upside down and the fruit fell off both of our trees. We didn't understand anything about each other except that we didn't understand each other. Our fights seemed monumental. And so was our frustration and anger. We would both get so upset at our inability to communicate and at our apparent "mistake of a lifetime," that we would both explode in anger. And in order to save our bedroom door and fine china, we both took action. Michael bought a punching bag, and I went to Goodwill and bought an armful of cheap plates. Our basement/garage was subterranean and covered with a thick rock wall. So we set up our "anger management" stations in the garage with a big pile of ceramic plates for me and a punching bag for him. Every time that we argued, which was almost every day, I would run downstairs and pick up a plate and scream as I sent it careening into the wall. The sensation of destruction and the outpouring of my anger on that fragile object would relieve enough stress for me so that I could return to the fray, get back to the relationship, and try to power through the next few hours. Ah, wedded bliss!

If anyone would have told us how hard it is to live with a human being of the opposite sex, we couldn't have believed them—we wouldn't have believed them. Before marriage, the fruitful life came easily; hope was the focus, dreams the delight, and fantasy the certainty. But after marriage the fruitful life stood in direct opposition to my feelings of bitterness, anger, doubt, and pain. And I came to realize that **the fruit of the Spirit doesn't show itself so much when life is a dream, when there is no chaffing, no trials, no suffering, and no compromise. What shows itself in those moments of perfection is the fruit of the flesh** seen in Romans 8:5: *"For those who live according to the flesh set their minds on the things of the flesh."* When I set my mind on the things of the flesh, and the things of the flesh are good, well then the fruit of that life is good as well. How easy it is to manifest love in your life when you've just fallen in love. How easy to be joyful when the future is so bright. How effortless are our kindness and goodness when love is new and warts are unseen. And so out of the satisfaction of my flesh came fruit that looked a lot like the fruit of the Spirit in me but was only the flesh in me in a moment of relationship perfection.

But marriage—marriage was totally different. Never before had the sin in my life been so exposed for another to see—and another's for me to see. Never had my love, patience, and faithfulness been so put to the test by my sinful nature. Never before had I seen my selfishness, fearfulness, and doubt so clearly as in the face and words of the new mirror in my life, my husband. And so for me, the Fruitful Wife becomes my biggest challenge ever. Living life with a man at my side, all the while manifesting the life of Christ in me in the face of my husband's faux pas, misunderstandings, rejections and failures, is impossible in the power of my flesh. I am unable to abandon my self-protection, self-importance, and self-obsession, especially when he's wrong, hurtful, or ignorant. I naturally resort to self when tested; it's my habit, my nature, my flesh. When I'm misunderstood, I get defensive. When I'm uncomfortable, I complain. When I'm tired, I'm cranky. When I'm at the end of my rope, I lack all self-control. So the descriptive, "Fruitful Wife," does not come naturally to me.

The Fruit of the Flesh

Maybe there are women who, when frustrated by their husband's laziness and failure to help out around the house, are patient and peaceful, but that's not my natural bent. Maybe there are women who, when their husbands reject their advances or accuse them of being selfish or unreliable, still act in love with self-control and kindness, but that's not my first instinct. Essentially whenever Michael points out, exposes, or in any way reminds me of my failure in life, i.e., my sinfulness, my first reaction is the opposite of fruitful. I want to respond with any combination of another kind of fruit, which I call **the nine fruit of the flesh: selfishness, joylessness, conflict, impatience, mercilessness, immorality, unfaithfulness, pride, and self-indulgence.** These come easily, but the nine fruit of the Spirit go against every fiber in my being. My flesh literally fights against them, making war in my heart and mind. In Romans 7 Paul identifies with this war: *"So I find it to be a law that when I want to do right, evil lies close at hand. For I delight in the law of God, in my inner being, but I see in my members another law waging war against the law of my mind and making me captive to the law of sin that dwells in my members"* (vv. 21–23).

I am not alone. This war is universal; it touches us all. And I believe that nowhere is it seen so forceful and tragic as in the relationship of husband and wife. A frightfully high number of Christian marriages end in divorce. Why? Because of this war that wages within. This battle between the flesh and the Spirit isn't spoken of as much as the symptoms of the battle are spoken of. Our feelings of betrayal, of hurt, of rejection, of abandonment, of isolation, and of frustration are often talked about, but they are not the cause or the root of the problem— only the symptoms. The root lies in our spiritual barrenness, our lack of the fruit of the Spirit. If we were abundant with this fruit, our arguments wouldn't have the sting they now carry, our suffering wouldn't be useless but useful, and rejection would drive us to our knees instead of to our attorneys. The Holy Spirit enters the life of the believer with all the power of God, because that's what he is: God the Holy Spirit dwelling inside each of us. And with that Spirit comes all that we need for life, faith, hope, and love. And out of the mere presence of his Spirit grows a fruit so sweet, so powerful, and so useful that nothing, neither death nor life, nor angels nor rulers, nor things present nor things to come, nor powers, nor height nor depth, nor anything else in all creation, can separate it from us. And nothing can separate us from him, our Lord and Savior.

THE UNBELIEVING HUSBAND. Many women live with unregenerate, unthankful, or unloving men, and the prospects for their lives seem bleak. But the prospects for their fruit are bright, because the Holy Spirit does not break or bend in the trials of life. He does not weaken or walk away when times get tough and love is lacking, but he holds on and never leaves you or forsakes you (Jer. 29:11). The barren, unproductive, and empty life is not meant for you. After all, God says, *"You did not choose me, but I chose you and appointed you that you should go and bear fruit and that your fruit should abide"* (John 15:16). **The actions or feelings of our men were never meant to be the deciding or controlling factor in our actions or feelings, but the opportunity for us to remember the life of Christ within us, allowing that life to produce fruit in keeping with our Savior.**

Abiding Fruit

The fruitful wife is not reliant on her own strength, abilities, or nature for the growth of fruit. And she isn't stuck within the confines of her personality or natural bent, unable to break free to the fruitfulness of more love, joy, peace, patience, kindness, faithfulness, goodness, and self-control. If any of those are as lacking in your nature, as I find them in mine, then thank God that he doesn't leave it all up to us, but the fruit of the Spirit is the manifestation of God the Holy Spirit in our lives. And so the prescription for a more fruitful life is the task of simply abiding in Christ. As Jesus explains of himself in John 15:5, *"I am the vine; you are the branches. Whoever abides in me and I in him, he it is that bears much fruit, for apart from me you can do nothing."*

So if the fruit of the Spirit is the manifestation of God the Holy Spirit in our lives, why does there even need to be a book on the subject? Why don't we just pray and trust God to give us the fruit? Why do we fail to be fruitful when we want it so badly, love him so much, and ask for it so diligently? Is there something wrong with us? The answer to that question is the reason for this work. The reason that *The Fruitful Wife* came into being is that without abiding in Christ by being mindful, without the knowledge of the nature of God and the fruit of his Spirit, we are less likely to respond to the circumstances of life with spiritual fruitfulness, regardless of how much we say we love him, beg him, or trust him. It is because of her lack of knowledge of who God is and what he's done that the believing woman finds it so hard to abide and trust in Christ and so to develop the fruit of the Spirit in her life. As we abide, we come to know more about him and his Word, and as this mindfulness grows, so does fruitfulness. A modern saying growing in popularity and used among Christian authors and pastors is "preach the gospel to yourself every day." This is a foundational example of being mindful daily of who you are, who God is, and what he has done. Charles Spurgeon agreed with this belief when he said that **"no sinner around you will be saved except by the knowledge of the great truths contained in the Word of God.** No man will ever be brought to repentance, to faith, and to life in Christ apart from the constant application of the truth through the Spirit." The life of Christ found in the Word of God is essential to the fruitful life. Without it we cannot be mindful of God's will in our lives; we aren't aware of his nature or of his purposes for his people. But as we remember to abide in Christ, and so increase our awareness and love for God's Word on the subject of the fruit of the Spirit, we can see more clearly the sin in the choices we once made and, instead, choose to abide rather than to wander or stray from his presence.

The reason Christ came was to give you life, and to give it to you abundantly (John 10:10). That abundance includes a life filled to overflowing with the fruit of the Spirit. Christ will do the work in you; he will give you peace for your worry, love for your fear, and joy for your sadness. All you have to do is "*trust in the* LORD *with all your heart, and do not lean on your own understanding. In all your ways acknowledge him, and he will make straight your paths*" (Prov. 3:5–6). If your life has been anything but fruitful, then fear not, because he will make good on his promise to work "*in you, both to will and to work for his good pleasure*" (Phil. 2:13).

In his book *Fruit of the Spirit*, G. W. Bethune states it more concisely and eloquently than I ever could when he says, "The mind, enlightened by the Holy Spirit, perceives and understands the truth; the conscience, quickened by the Holy Spirit, feels and acknowledges it; the heart, converted by the Holy Spirit, loves and obeys it."[1]

The big question, then, is can you truly bear fruit if you aren't abiding? I know many nonbelievers who love, who are kind, gentle, patient, and joyful. They love their families, they help their friends, and they serve the world, sometimes better than believers, but only because it feels good. Their fruit grows because of the payoff they receive. A woman might love a man because of how he makes her feel, how he looks, or how much money he makes. People might give because of how important it makes them feel or how much it relieves their guilt. People do things for lots of reasons, but whatever does not come from the Spirit, but from the flesh, is done out of pleasure seeking. In other words, when the flesh is our source of fruit, the motivation isn't God's glory but our own. So, even those who seem so selfless and good can be, at the root of it all, just serving themselves. And while it can be beneficial and kind, it isn't evidence of the life of the Spirit or its fruit, because its ultimate goal is glorifying self and not God.

We must understand that without the life of Christ in us, any fruit worth producing is not sustainable. When hard times hit, when tempers fly, when necessity demands it, the fruit produced by sheer brute strength falters, because it isn't the produce of the Spirit but of the flesh attempting to please itself. For most of us, any study of the fruit of the Spirit draws us inward and forces us to look at our lives, emotions, or feelings. We examine our lives for love, joy, or self-control and see that we sorely lack what we desperately need. We want more fruit, but we can't seem to find it. What are we missing? Perhaps a better understanding of the purpose of the fruit of the Spirit will shed some light on its absence in your life. Have you considered the idea of the tree? It does not grow fruit for itself but to give it to those who would take it from its branches. Fruit doesn't satisfy the tree from which it grows; it is meant to give glory to the husbandman or gardener and to benefit those who have need of its fruit. So it is with your fruit, which is meant for "*the common good,*" we read in 1 Corinthians 12:7. You cannot consider the purpose of the fruit of the Spirit to be your happiness but the glory of God and the hope, faith, and life of others. Your fruit is meant to serve the hungry, to prove the goodness of the Spirit from which it comes to those who would partake of it. Though there is no question of a residual benefit associated with experiencing the fruit of the Spirit—its ultimate goal is to serve the gardener by feeding those who have access to its fruit.

So the fruit of the Spirit isn't about pleasure or pleasing self at all, but about denying self and giving all to the glory to God. It's about needing nothing for ourselves from the fruit we produce. It's truly unconditional, meant to serve the will of God. This fruit comes not from the goodness of our hearts but from the goodness of the Spirit of God, who lives in our hearts. By becoming mindful of abiding in Christ and desiring to respond to the Spirit's promptings rather than to our flesh, we set our minds on the things of the Spirit rather than the things of the flesh, and when that happens our fruit begins to flourish.

I can tell you from experience that what I lacked in the area of fruitfulness wasn't due to God's lacking but to my misunderstanding of his power and nature and my inability to be mindful of remaining in Christ in my everyday thoughts and actions. What I tend to do is live life as it is dealt to me, reacting out of my emotional center, a place that not only makes the most sense to me but also speaks highly of me and seems to have my best interests at heart. Daily I have given lip service to Christ but based my decisions on myself. But I have found great relief from much of my self by learning to abide through seeking to better understand the fruit of that abiding. It is my prayer that you also, through yearning to abide and so diving into a deeper knowledge of the words of Galatians 5:22–23, will find your life to be more fruitful than you had ever imagined it could be.

With this in mind, *The Fruitful Wife* will attempt to open the eyes of the reader to a deeper understanding of the fruit of the Spirit and how it shows itself in a woman's life, especially in marriage. In each chapter we will dive into the notion of abiding and of better understanding the fruit of the Spirit, found in Galatians 5:22–23, and talk about how when we remain in Christ, focused on him and his Word, the Spirit has his way with us and grows fruit in abundance. It is my hope that, as you start to better understand the biblical meaning of words such as *love*, *peace*, and *joy*, that you will begin to see areas in your life in which you have, maybe even unknowingly, chosen their opposite and begin to see the areas where the Spirit is guiding you to choose differently in the future. Through a more thorough understanding of the words used to describe a fruitful life, you may very well find the Spirit revealing areas in your life where you have unknowingly adopted the fruit of the flesh and be enlightened to the power of abiding in Christ.

But the fruit of the Spirit is
LOVE

LOVE

The Spirit is indeed nothing less than the Divine Love itself come down to dwell in us, and that we have only so much of the Spirit as we have of Love.

—ANDREW MURRAY

Love must ever give to its own, whatever the cost.

—A. W. TOZER

When I was growing up, the words "I love you" were rarely spoken in my family. While most kids hear them each night as they are tucked into bed, I was told that to say them too often would cheapen them. This was the general mood of my childhood. While my parents were very kind, generous, and good, they had little understanding of love, and so they passed that ignorance on to me. Affection was rare, not only between my parents and me but also between my parents themselves. I rarely saw any confirmations, expressions, or feelings of love expressed between them, and my parents' marriage would eventually end in divorce.

I Love Big Macs

Because love wasn't modeled in my home, I grew up understanding the word as the way to define good experiences or feelings. I learned to say things like "I love horses," "I love Big Macs," and "I love watching TV," but I seldom expressed love for people. It wasn't until I started to have strong feelings for boys that I got the urge to say "I love you" to another human being. With this emotional and hormonal change, my ideas of love began to grow. I soon came to view love as an intense feeling for another human being emanating from physical desire. My understanding of love stayed in this space for most of my early adult life, helping me to decide that love is fleeting, that it hurts tremendously, and that it is almost impossible to find. I gave my heart for short periods of time, soon to recant in favor of a new object of affection, as I went from man to man.

Love never really found form in my life, not until my true love came along in the person of Jesus. When I started to see what true love is, when I took a look at the Author of love, I started to get a more accurate, wholesome, and beneficial understanding of this seemingly unfathomable concept. According to God's Word, much to my surprise, love is less about how I feel, but more about what I do. It isn't about getting, but giving. It isn't about reward, but sacrifice. And it isn't about excitement, but endurance.

In the chapter of Scripture most recited at weddings, 1 Corinthians 13, we are given a godly description of a love lived not for self but for the loved one. A love that sees the object of its affection delights in that object and wants nothing but the other's welfare, even over self. In God's own words, *"Love is patient and kind; love does not envy or boast; it is not arrogant or rude. It does not insist on its own way; it is not irritable or resentful; it does not rejoice at wrongdoing, but rejoices with the truth. Love bears all things, believes all things, hopes all things, endures all things. Love never ends"* (1 Cor. 13:4–8). If you look closely at this list of characteristics of love, you will see something striking, which is that it's got the fruit of the Spirit all over it. Patience and kindness are listed first. Goodness is a part of not being *irritable* or *resentful*. Gentleness is wrapped up in *"it is not arrogant or rude."* Joy is a part of *rejoicing with the truth.* Faithfulness is revealed in the words *"bears all things, believes all things."* And peace is seen in *"does not insist on its own way."* The only thing we can't immediately spot here is self-control; however, each of these responses to being tested by our loved ones requires some form of self-control.

So then, we can see that love is not just another fruit of the Spirit; it is the foundation of all of the fruit, a requirement, an essential first fruit before all others. And conversely, without each of the fruit, love would be nonexistent. Without love, all other fruit will be a cheap imitation of the real thing. As it says at the beginning of 1 Corinthians 13 about this kind of love-less goodness, "*If I speak in the tongues of men and of angels, but have not love, I am a noisy gong or a clanging cymbal. And if I have prophetic powers, and understand all myster-ies and all knowledge, and if I have all faith, so as to remove mountains, but have not love, I am nothing. If I give away all I have, and if I deliver up my body to be burned, but have not love, I gain nothing*" (vv. 1–3). So then, the other fruit of the Spirit done without love are useless, nothing, a vapor in the wind.

Love Is Not Just a Feeling

Most of us grow up thinking that love is romance and ecstasy. We hear the words "You complete me," and we melt into a puddle of emotional goo. We understand that love is more than just feelings, but when those feelings of love are gone, we usually assume that love has gone as well, or perhaps was never there, because we are convinced in our heart of hearts that love is a feeling, and a very good one at that. But God's Word says nothing of the sort.

In 1975 the rock band Nazareth produced a hit song, "Love Hurts," and since then it has been the anthem of bro-ken hearts across the globe. The truth is that love does hurt our selves, because **love, if purely lived, strips us of all our self-interest, self-promotion, and self-protection.** Love is bound to cause pain to our flesh, because it doesn't serve self but those it loves. That is why love is so hard and why so many of us fail at it time and again, because of our idea that love is meant to serve the lover instead of the loved one. Add that with the somewhat subconscious idea that love is all feeling, and together we have a hot mess. Love as it was never meant to be made.

But according to God's Word, love is something altogether different. If love were simply a feeling, God could not command it, at least not without equipping us to fulfill it. Feelings are not something that can be easily turned on and off. I cannot command you to feel fear or to feel elation; you can't generate these on command. It would be a cruel God who would command you to do something you are incapable of doing. But, as you know, God is good, not cruel, and so here is the secret to loving the unlovable: we are able to love those the world finds difficult because of God's great and all-encompassing love for us. When we love God with our all, his love pours out of us onto others in ways impossible for our flesh. So we are able to obey Jesus's commands to love our enemies, to pray for those who persecute us, and to refuse to fight back or seek revenge because our love is an action in response to how he first loved us (Matt. 5:39, 44). So love must first be understood as dependent on his love for us, and our response to love must be action, not reliance on feeling good.

Growing up believing that love is all about emotions had put me into bondage to those emotions. I was taken hostage each time someone assaulted my feelings, broke my heart, or rejected me. I was a slave to how I felt in relationship to other human beings rather than free to love, regardless of return. But when I discovered this one simple truth about love, and that real love is content not to feel good all the time, I was able to give the kind of love that the Father had given to me, a love not found in what man does or doesn't do, but in who God is. After all, *"God shows his love for us in that while we were still sinners, Christ died for us"* (Rom. 5:8). We are indwelt with this kind of love when the Holy Spirit comes to live in us. And this is the kind of love we are able to give through the power of that Holy Spirit, as we read in Romans 5:5: "*God's love has been poured into our hearts through the Holy Spirit who has been given to us.*" It is through this power only that we are able to love without pretense or deception, without pretending that we are loving when what we are really doing is responding to the good feelings we get from the relationships in our lives, and without lying to ourselves that we can love only when others love us in return. When you love wrongly, Jesus says, "*what reward do you have? Do not even the tax collectors do the same? And if you greet only your brothers, what more are you doing than others? Do not even the Gentiles do the same?*" (Matt 5:46–48). **So love is not about responding to how others make us feel but about the Holy Spirit's promptings in our souls.**

CONFESSIONS OF A SELFISH WOMAN. I am not good at loving anyone but myself. I am always my first thought, my first purpose; even before my own child I think of myself. It is not natural for me to love others first, so I'm not suggesting that I have arrived, or that I am selfless—quite the opposite. And so it is a daily reckoning that I must do, reminding myself of God's love for me, and the love that he wants me to give to others as a way to not only love them but him as well. May we all learn to turn our minds to the love of God daily so that we may love others the way that he has loved us.

If you take a close look at the love description in 1 Corinthians 13, you will notice that it is not a feel-good passage. It doesn't encourage good feelings, but hard ones. It doesn't command emotion, but swift and difficult action in the face of frustration. It is, after all, only frustrating or difficult people that require patience. And with those who bring out our envy and competitiveness, love demands the opposite. When others want something we don't want, when we are at odds, love doesn't insist on its own way. When people push our buttons, love isn't irritable. When they hurt us, it isn't resentful. Are you seeing the pattern in this love passage? The love defined in God's Word is all about responding in an unnatural but supernatural way to difficult and challenging people. So, the love defined in God's Word is not focused on self, but on denying self.

This is another thing we have to be reminded of as we study the idea of love, that **it requires selflessness.** Not surprising, since part of living by the Spirit means putting ourselves to death, as we read in Romans 8:13: *"For if you live according to the flesh you will die, but if by the Spirit you put to death the deeds of the body, you will live."* It is through putting to death our need to feel love and embracing our Spirit-led desire to give love that we start to experience this first and most important piece of the fruit of the Spirit. The study of love has to move away from feelings, requirements, and self-centered thinking and move toward Spirit and truth.

The Opposite of Love

If you ask most people what the opposite of love is, they would probably say hate. That makes sense, but it's not necessarily the best answer. Believing that love is lacking only when there is hatred is a dangerous notion that can lead to all kinds of pain and struggle.

I once counseled a woman who was having great difficulties in her marriage. Her husband was cold and distant, and she was at her wits' end as to what to do. So we began to meet to talk about her life from God's perspective. As I asked her questions and heard her complaints, I started to see a pattern. Her husband's biggest complaint was her continual yelling at her kids, which ruined the peaceful nature of his home. Every morning she screamed at the kids as she rushed to get them ready for school, and every night she screamed at them to clean up and get ready for bed, and her husband was turned off by all of her yelling. I told her the first thing she had to do was to quit yelling, but that didn't help; she continued to yell for yet another week. As we met again, I started to dig deeper, and as she told me that her kids were always disobedient and messy, I started to see the problem. "I know what it is," I told her one day. "What?" she asked eagerly. "You don't love your kids. You love yourself." "That's not true!" she adamantly responded. She was right by the world's definition of love, but I wanted her to see that although she might feel love for them, she wasn't expressing love for them, and therefore it wasn't love at all. Since all her actions were based on what she was feeling and wanting, her actual condition was one of selfishness. I went on to read her 1 Corinthians 13 and allowed her to apply it to her short-tempered, frustrated, record-keeping, selfish relationship with her kids.

"Does that sound like love to you?" I asked her. She was mortified. She had never looked at the actions of love as God defines it in direct relationship to her own life. She had never taken a real and self-assessing look at love from the outside in, and that was why there was so much strife, fighting, and bitterness in her household.

After taking a sober look at God's definition of love, she was able to apply it to her life and to change the culture of her home. Within a week, everything was different. The shouting stopped, the kids started to obey, and incredibly her husband started to soften toward her. This wasn't because of the effort she exerted but because of her new awareness of the life of Christ in her and his selfless love for her.

For weeks, months even, she had tried, through her own effort, to gain control of her emotions, to care for her kids without yelling, and to love her husband the way he wanted to be loved. She had known what she was doing was wrong, but she was powerless to stop. Why? Because she didn't have the Spirit in her? No, I believe she was filled with the Holy Spirit, but she was not mindful of that Spirit within her. But once she became utterly mindful of the life of Christ within her, of his Word and his will, she was able to change what was essentially self-obsession to true love. Instead of reading 1 Corinthians 13 as something to get, she now read it as a command to live out, one that the Spirit had equipped her to do. It has been my experience in talking with women that the quickest way to make a change in their lives is to become aware of the nature of the Spirit and his thoughts on the life of faith.

Understanding love is essential in the pursuit of love. Without this knowledge of who God is and how he loves us, we cannot express or experience true love, and without an understanding of what love *isn't*, we can't truly eradicate the areas in our lives where love is lacking. It is important, then, to realize that **the opposite of love isn't hate, but selfishness.** Thinking that the opposite of love is hate allows us to ignore the lack of love in our lives because it feels nothing like hate. I have found that most of the women I talk to about marriage problems have a list of requirements on love that are seen nowhere in Scripture. They have an unwritten writ, their own law, that they subconsciously believe has to be obeyed in order for love to be found in a relationship.

When this self-created law is broken by our husbands, we feel at liberty to judge and even punish them. When our husbands don't like our meals, when they comment on the messy house, when they don't wine and dine us on our anniversary, we see that as disobedience to our law of self, and we retaliate. This is the practical working out of a life that involves self in the definition of love. **Whenever our well-being, happiness, or hope is wrapped up in what another person says or does, we are not living the love of 1 Corinthians 13, and we most definitely are not living life from the Spirit but from the flesh.** The act of biblical love is kind. It is caring, friendly, sympathetic, tender, and unselfish. The acts of the flesh are disinterested, detached, disapproving, cold, and argumentative. These are the exact opposite of biblical love and stand in direct defiance of the life of the Spirit that is inside us. **When the men we love disobey what we believe they should be obeying, be it God's Word or our own, and we react with disapproval, disinterest, or arguments, then we are not acting in love, because each of these unbiblical responses is an antonym to love.** While they are natural, human responses to conflict or pain, they are not biblical responses, and therefore they are not fruitful or obedient.

Why Is Love Commanded?

Love is the foundational evidence of the fruit of the Spirit, but it is also a biblical command. There are many reasons why God commands us to love one another, and at least five seem to stand out as the most obvious.

The first is the most important, which is that God is love. In 1 John 4:16 we read the most essential words on love in the Bible: "*God is love, and whoever abides in love abides in God, and God abides in him.*" What does this short but important statement mean and how do we make sense of it? In answering this, I turn to John Piper, who answers beautifully when he says:

God is love. In a word I think it means something like: God's absolute fullness of life and truth and beauty and goodness and all other perfections is such that he is not only self-sufficient, but also, in his very nature, overflowing. God is so absolute, so perfect, so complete, so full, so inexhaustibly resourceful, so joyful, that he is by nature a Giver, a Worker for others, a Helper, a Protector. What it means to be God is to be full enough always to overflow and never to need—never murmur, never pout. God is love. The implications of this for the way we live are big.[2]

Big is right, and in Ephesians 5:1–2 we see just how big the implications for each of us are when we are called to *"be imitators of God, as beloved children. And walk in love, as Christ loved us and gave himself up for us, a fragrant offering and sacrifice to God."*

Since God's very nature is love, it would stand to reason that those he calls "children" would have that same nature, just as our earthly children have our own nature. So, we love not only because our Father is love and we are his children, but, **second, because he has loved us.** In 1 John 4:11–12, the command to love is explained this way: *"Beloved, if God so loved us, we also ought to love one another. No one has ever seen God; if we love one another, God abides in us and his love is perfected in us."* We don't love to be loved in return but because this is how God has loved us. When we are given something, God expects us to give the same. We aren't meant to be black holes of his love, ever sucking in and never overflowing; we are meant to be the evidence of his love as we give what we ourselves have been given, undeserved and unmerited. Remembering what we have been forgiven serves to allow us to love others who must also be forgiven and loved regardless of their merit.

This leads to **the third reason why God commands us to love, and that is in order to love him in return.** Loving God isn't just about your relationship with him, your intimacy and spiritual connectedness, but it is also about loving others as you love yourself. We see this in Jesus's response to a question found in Matthew: *"Teacher, which is the great commandment in the Law?"* When asked what is the most important thing to God, Jesus's reply was this: *"You shall love the Lord your God with all your heart and with all your soul and with all your mind. This is the great and first commandment. And a second is like it: You shall love your neighbor as yourself. On these two commandments depend all the Law and the Prophets"* (Matt. 22:36–41).

So, loving God requires everything that is within us—all our heart, soul, and mind. Everything in us is to be focused on loving God. But Jesus follows that commandment with the second, and that is to love your neighbor as yourself. This is not possible if you don't love God with your all, with absolute surrender. In fact, since Jesus included this second command, it can be said that we cannot fully love God if we do not love his children. John drives the point home with these vital words on loving God: *"If anyone says, 'I love God,' and hates his brother, he is a liar; for he who does not love his brother whom he has seen cannot love God whom he has not seen. And this commandment we have from him: whoever loves God must also love his brother"* (1 John 4:20–21). So, loving God means loving others. There is no option. **A woman who says she loves God must act in love to her neighbor in order to demonstrate her love for God.**

If you are like me, you might have just let out an anxious sigh, because that's a tall order. Loving God is the easy part. He is perfect; he never makes a mistake. He is a faithful, good, kind, generous, wise God. What isn't there to love? But man has a few faults. And when we add those faults to our own faults, we've got a messy relationship and a love challenge. But the realization that love isn't just a feeling but also an action, and that if we love God, we will love others, isn't meant to convict us when we fail to love perfectly but to encourage us to be mindful of the Spirit that lives in us, of his nature, power, and his plans for us.

When Jesus gave a "new commandment" to his disciples after having washed their feet, including those of Judas, the one who would betray him, he said, *"A new commandment I give to you, that you love one another: just as I have loved you, you also are to love one another. By this all people will know that you are my disciples, if you have love for one another"* (John 13:34–35). **We are commanded by God to love one another so that the world will know that we are his.** Can you imagine the witness of a woman who showed no love for her husband, who belittled, controlled, dishonored, and complained about him? What of God would the world see in that? How could she draw others to the One who saves when she acts like the one who destroys? God's children must love each other in order that they can be known to the world.

Finally, God commands love because it is important for us. **By obeying God's commands to love—by following after love with all our heart, soul, and mind—we are perfected.** We see this in the words penned by John through the Holy Spirit: *"By this we know that we have come to know him, if we keep his commandments. Whoever says 'I know him' but does not keep his commandments is a liar, and the truth is not in him, but whoever keeps his word, in him truly the love of God is perfected"* (1 John 2:3–5). Did you catch that? We don't obey God's commands to love so that we can get love but so that we can be *perfected*! The love of God is perfected in us when we love not just the lovable but the unlovely, the cruel, the difficult, the forgetful. God binds everything together into perfect harmony through love (Col. 3:14).

We love because God, who is love, first loved us. And we show our love to God by our love to man. If our love for God were perfect, so would our love for others be. While I will be the first to say that my love for God is not perfect, perfect love is my goal. It is through being ever mindful of the Spirit of God in me, the Spirit of love, and this abiding, that I turn my gaze away from my flesh, which demands justice, respect, hearing, and honor, and toward my God, who is all-sufficient even when I am often insufficient.

Loving Your Man

So then, in the strength of the Spirit, how do you love sinful man? What are the practical ways that love shows up in our relationships, and how do we let the Spirit teach us to love? These are the questions we have to ask when it comes to being a fruitful woman, because a fruitful woman will first of all be overflowing with the fruit of love.

Consider Him More Significant

So let's take a look from God's own words at what love in marriage looks like when we allow the Spirit to feed it. First, as the Fruitful Wife responds to the Spirit she begins to consider her husband more significant than herself. Stop! Don't throw the book down and jump on it, especially if you're reading on an iPad. I know that may be your urge. How can a woman swallow the thought that she ought to consider her husband more significant than herself? That's appalling and weak, but those aren't my words. I'm not the one that came up with them, or I would swiftly recant them, but they are God's words found in the book of Philippians: "*Do nothing from selfish ambition or conceit, but in humility count others more significant than yourselves*" (2:3). Nine times out of ten, I'm not doing this. Nine times out of ten (and that's being generous), I'm thinking that I'm more significant than my husband. I'm thinking, *Why is he not doing this, or that? It would be kind, loving, or healthier for me.* Nine times out of ten it's all about me, and my world, and how he's affecting it, not him and his, and that's what's appalling. That's where I'm loving out of my flesh and not out of the Spirit, and it's the foundation for all the trouble in my relationship.

At the point that we fail to humble ourselves in any area of life, we have a problem, because we are living out of the center of our flesh. We tend to only do things that feel natural, but as the Spirit becomes the source of our love, considering others more important will begin to feel supernatural. And as that happens situations that used to lead us to argument and strife, sadness and dejection, will be replaced by a love that only the Spirit could implant, a love that fearlessly abandons itself to the glory of God through the love of his children.

Humble Yourself

It is out of humility that the ability to truly love comes, because humility takes us off the throne of our lives and puts God there. Humility makes life no longer about us but about him, and for that to happen it must be in relationship to his children, especially to the child he has assigned as our mate. We could devote volumes to the topic of humility, but here I'll list just a few ways that the Spirit manifests humility in the relationship of marriage.

Turn the Other Cheek

The Holy Spirit compels us to **consider others more significant than self, and when that happens our notion of justice shifts.** In Matthew 5:38 Jesus says this: *"You have heard that it was said, 'An eye for an eye and a tooth for a tooth.'"* This Old Testament idea is practical and sensible in a life lived for and through the flesh, but Jesus rejects this idea in favor of a more humble notion when he says, *"But I say to you, Do not resist the one who is evil. But if anyone slaps you on the right cheek, turn to him the other also"* (Matt. 5:39).

Maybe you have made retaliation a part of your creed in relationship to your husband. When he says or does something that hurts you, you want nothing more than to make him squirm. You want to prove and defend yourself and win the argument, but that is living by the flesh, not by the Spirit. Living for love and not for vindication in the relationship of marriage is a requirement. Sure, there are marriages where this concept isn't acceptable to the wife, and in those marriages one of two things happens. Either the husband obeys Jesus's command to turn the other cheek while waiting for his wife to love biblically, or the husband joins in with the wife in his refusal to obey the law of love, and the marriage is destroyed.

Don't Allow His Sin to Be an Excuse for Yours

When our marriage is in disarray, when we wonder where the love has gone, we need look no further than ourselves and our inability to remain in Christ by trusting God's Word to be good for us and essential for love. When the Fruitful Wife senses her husband becoming more of an enemy than a friend, the Spirit within her reminds her that his sin is no excuse for hers. When her love for Christ is deep, it overwhelms her pain and anger at the sight of a loveless husband. As she abides in Christ and rests in the trust of his sufficiency, her instinct for self-protection subsides and the fruit of love is grown.

God has left us all with a reminder, with encouragement when things get rough in relationship. In 1 Peter 2:23 we read of Christ that "*when he was reviled, he did not revile in return; when he suffered, he did not threaten, but continued entrusting himself to him who judges justly.*" And as we abide in Christ, the Spirit brings things like this to mind, redirecting our wrath and channeling our injustice into trust in the One who judges justly.

Don't Take His Sin Personally

The guidance of God can't be avoided or rejected by the child of God (see Heb. 10:26). That is complete defiance and self-worship and it says, "I know better than God, and I'm going to do it my way." Far better, and the way to turn the other cheek, is to **never take your husband's sin personally.** When you take it personally, it becomes all about you, but the truth is that his sin is all about his relationship with God. It is God's law, not yours, that he has broken, and it is that relationship that must be rebuilt. Once that relationship is reconciled, so will yours be. To take his sin personally is to invite sin into your own life.

Whenever I take Michael's sin personally, I find myself suffering from the sin of resentment, bitterness, and even hate. There are times when my perfect Michael, being human, sins, as surprising as that may be, and in those moments, if I take it personally I feel the full brunt of his sin on my emotions, and I am not strong enough to handle the weight. It tears at my heart and weakens my soul, and I want nothing more than to make it stop by teaching him the error of his ways. But this never ends well.

When our husband sins, the most important thing a Fruitful Wife can do is not react until she is sure that she is out of the equation. In other words, she must make sure her reaction isn't out of self-protection or self-interest, which spells sin. It's important that our motive in every relationship is never self, but the Father. We bear the fruit of the Spirit when we react out of that Spirit.

When your husband sins, the best answer is always prayer. There may be times when a wife shares her spiritual insight with her husband, but, like disciplining a child, it must *not* be done when she is angry, resentful, bitter, or hurting. This kind of reaction to sin leads only to more sin. Instead, the Fruitful

Wife calls on the Spirit and allows him to do the work in both her and her husband.

We cannot rush into correcting him, teaching him, or fighting with him, but we must know our husband—his heart, personality, and needs. Love seeks the best for the loved one, so the Fruitful Wife makes a study of her husband, learning his moods and reactions, so that she can be wise in her dealings with his sinful actions. She knows when it's the best time to talk to him about his sin, if at all. She knows how he deals with correction or discussions of his weaknesses. She knows when to pick her moments and how to be most effective in her actions. In other words, she knows what conditions make for a fruitful discussion!

I don't know how many times my temper has flared and my feelings have demanded justice, but miraculously in the Spirit I have refused them and instead walked away to a quiet place to beg the Father for help in my heart. Without fail the Father has come through. Ten times out of ten my prayers have been answered. Our marriage has improved and our sin has been revealed in the light of his presence. To take our husband's sin personally, and to take measures to correct him so that we can see justice, would be to take steps backward in the walk of faith and forward in the way of fruitlessness.

Respect and Honor

Another way God provides for a woman to love her husband is to respect and honor him (see Rom. 12:10; Eph. 5:33). To respect your husband is to treat him with kindness, trust, and honor. It is to appreciate him for being a man, someone different from you. It is to admire his manliness and to point that out. To respect him is to refuse to defy him, complain about him, or talk badly about him, especially in front of others. To honor him is to be quick to listen (see James 1:19–20) and to choose love with the descriptors of 1 Corinthians 13 without fail. It is not to insist on getting your own way. It is keeping no record of wrong. It is not coming in behind him to "fix" something he has done wrong. To honor your husband is a difficult if not impossible task in the flesh. It wars against self at every instance—believe me, I know—but **marriage is a unique institution that allows us the opportunity to die to ourselves, perhaps more than in any other way.** Giving honor and respect to your husband, especially when he doesn't deserve it, might be the most perfecting thing you will ever do, and it will point to your faith in God, whose covenant you live under.

Loving your husband isn't about being in love with him but about serving him. You aren't your husband's servant; you are God's servant. And you serve God through your service to others. Jesus explained it this way: "*Whoever would be great among you must be your servant, and whoever would be first among you must be slave of all. For even the Son of Man came not to be served but to serve, and to give his life as a ransom for many*" (Mark 10:43–45). There is no one closer to you than your husband, so, as you seek to serve God, the first place to start is with your man. The woman that serves prays for her husband religiously—not just occasionally, but daily, continually lifting him up and setting him before the Father. She also displays the fruit of the Spirit in relationship to her man. In relationship to her husband, the Fruitful Wife will see evidence of the fruit of the Spirit growing day by day.

Submit

When I first got married my biggest fear was this word, *submission*, which I hated. What I didn't get was that this word describes the fruitful life, the life that doesn't please the flesh but the Spirit, reacting to others in love, joy, peace, patience, kindness, goodness, faithfulness, gentleness, and self-control. It can be easy to stand on our rights, needs, and wants, especially when we have previously taken care of and looked out for ourselves. We are problem solvers and quick thinkers, and we know what's best for us and our families, but for some reason God doesn't want us to act on what comes naturally. The desires of the flesh come naturally; the desires of the Spirit, supernaturally.

Love also includes a love of God's Word and obedience to it. In 1 John 5:2–3 we are told that we can know we have love *"when we love God and obey his commandments. For this is the love of God, that we keep his commandments."* To love God is to obey. And one of the hardest commands to obey is: *"Wives, submit to your own husbands, as to the Lord"* (Eph. 5:22). To submit, in it's most feared sense, is to yield, back down, cave in, capitulate, surrender, or knuckle under. In its most basic sense, it is to be governed by or subject to another, to agree to what he asks, even when it isn't what we want. This is something our flesh does not want to do.

While submission may appear to be an ugly concept, it is a biblical one, and we must find beauty in it, as we do in all of God's words. In fact, our husband is commanded to lay down his life for his wife as Christ did for the church. What a burden! We are, after all, not really submitting to a man but to God, who has asked us to submit to him. Remember that your submission is to the Perfect One, who would ask you to do nothing that would be bad for you.

* * *

Holy Spirit love doesn't come naturally. The fruit of the flesh might look a good deal like the fruit of the Spirit—it might feel like it and sound like it—but **the fruit of the flesh always destroys and disappoints.** The Fruitful Wife accepts whatever worldly grief love may bring, resisting the temptation to destroy love through conditional and man-made law, and gives even though she may get nothing in return. The kind of love that the Holy Spirit provides to one who depends on him is the same kind of love that God the Father showed to each of us by giving up his only Son for our salvation. Although none of us deserved it, we have all been provided with it in deeper measure than we could ever know.

If you haven't loved in Spirit and truth but in flesh and doubt, it isn't too late to change. In relationship to your husband the road to recovery may be long, but it can be taken one step at a time, day by day, acknowledging the love that God teaches you through his Spirit. Allow yourself to be redeemed and remade into his likeness. It is never too late to grow the fruit of the Spirit in your life. There is no mistake too big that disqualifies you from love. Every one of us has lived and loved selfishly, but we have no reason to expect things to stay the same.

This "fruit of the Spirit" love is available to all who not only love God but also lean on him for his power and believe that his Word is true. God is love, and he could not love you more. So draw on that everlasting love as you love others, not for how it makes you feel but for his glory and a demonstration of his grace. Trust in the Author of your love to teach and help you to love as only he can love.

But the fruit of the Spirit is
JOY

2 JOY

*I have found that my lack of joy firmly rests on
my inability to consistently agree with God.*

—HAYLEY DIMARCO

Fleas—the place was swarming with fleas. The claustrophobic
rows of platform beds, three rows high that filled Barracks 28
at Ravensbruck concentration camp would be the new home
of Betsie and her sister Corrie ten Boom. After being arrested
for aiding the Jews during the Nazi invasion of Holland, both
sisters were sent off to this pit of despair to live out their lives
in darkness and pain. The conditions were subhuman. They
were packed into rooms with hundreds of other women,
forced to sleep on reeking straw palettes with not even enough
room to sit up. They lived with fleas, filth, and incredible sickness and were left without the comfort of blankets, pillows, or
even warmth.

*"How can we live in such a place?" Corrie begged her
sister. "Show us. Show us how," said Betsie matter-of-factly.
For Betsie, the distinction between prayer and the rest of life
seemed to be vanishing.*

*"Corrie!" she said excitedly. "He's given us the answer!
Read that part again!"*

*Corrie glanced down the long, dim aisle to make sure no
guard was in sight then drew the Bible from its pouch. "It was
First Thessalonians," she said. In the feeble light she turned
the pages. "Here it is: 'Comfort the frightened, help the weak,
be patient with everyone. See that none of you repays evil
for evil, but always seek to do good to one another and to
all . . .'" It seemed written expressly to Ravensbruck.*

"Go on," said Betsie. "That wasn't all."

"Oh yes: '. . . To one another and to all. Rejoice always, pray constantly, give thanks in all circumstances; for this is the will of God in Christ Jesus.'"

"That's it, Corrie! That's His answer. 'Give thanks in all circumstances!' That's what we can do. We can start right now to thank God for every single thing about this new barracks!"

Corrie stared at her, then around her at the dark, foul-aired room.

"Such as?" she said.

"Such as being assigned here together."

Corrie bit her lip. "Oh yes, Lord Jesus!"

"Such as what you're holding in your hands."

She looked down at the Bible. "Yes! Thank You, dear Lord, that there was no inspection when we entered here! Thank You for all the women, here in this room, who will meet You in these pages."

"Yes," said Betsie. "Thank You for the very crowding here. Since we're packed so close, that many more will hear!" She looked at me expectantly. "Corrie!" she prodded.

"Oh, all right. Thank You for the jammed, crammed, stuffed, packed, suffocating crowds."

"Thank You," Betsie went on serenely, "for the fleas and for . . ."

The fleas! This was too much. "Betsie, there's no way even God can make me grateful for the fleas."

"Give thanks in all circumstances," she quoted. "It doesn't say, 'in pleasant circumstances.' Fleas are part of this place where God has put us."

And so they stood between tiers of bunks and gave thanks for the fleas.[3]

The Joy of Fleas

A prerequisite for experiencing joy isn't a lack of pain, suffering, or grief. *"Count it all joy . . . when you meet trials of many kinds,"* says James 1:2. No one better understood the capacity for joy in the midst of trials than Corrie ten Boom, who later was able to call her time at Ravensbruck joyful. That would be unthinkable to modern man and unconceivable to those who don't know the amazing joy that comes to those of us who not only know God but have his Holy Spirit living and working inside of us.

Joy can feel a lot like happiness. It can make you smile and give you hope. But it has a different nature than happiness, a different source. Happiness, like the sun and rain, comes to the faithful and the unfaithful alike (see Matt. 5:45). Its nature is to find release in blessing, perfection, comfort, and ease. Happiness results from good circumstances. It is a wonderful thing in anyone's life, but it is fragile, reliant on the weather, the relationship, or success. Happiness cannot honestly be realized in the midst of sorrow, pain, or suffering. It requires a just-right environment to flourish, and that is why no one is continuously happy. There are always moments that disappoint, moments that test and try.

Joy, on the other hand, is reliant on the perfect nature of the Creator. Joy can survive devastation, loss, and injury. It can survive interruption, irritation, and fatigue. Its supernatural origin, found in the Holy Spirit, makes it an unfathomable fruit that defies all odds and rewards those who remain mindful of its source.

But joy isn't something that comes naturally to us, certainly not when things become increasingly difficult. In those moments, asking joy to take center stage in your heart is like asking water to come out of a rock, and truth be told, the fruit of the Spirit can seem like this, especially in the area of joy. Feelings are hard to manipulate, hard to generate out of thin air, so being commanded to "*rejoice always*" (1 Thess. 5:16) sounds impossible. Yet the lives of women like Betsie and Corrie tell us differently. How, when feelings argue against the very idea of rejoicing, do we do the opposite of what we feel? First, we have to understand that to rejoice is to do something, not to feel something. Joy is consummated not with the heart but with the voice. Happiness celebrates how we feel, but we can rejoice over what we know is true regardless of feeling. Joy is the realization that we no longer have to live under our own power. The expression of thanks and the vocalization of delight and hope for a greater purpose that we know nothing of is fullness of joy. In that dark prison ward, the ten Boom sisters felt a pleasure not in the fleas but in the God who allowed them. They rejoiced not in the hunger and sickness but in the God who never forgets or rejects those who love him and seek his face.

Joy is not just the experience but the sight. When we are mindful of God's Word, he is gracious and gives us spiritual sight. It is seeing the hand of God in all circumstances of your life, knowing that his Word is no less true and his goodness no less good because things look and feel bleak, and then being able to vocalize that truth and share that joy. This is why Paul prays that God "*may give you the Spirit of wisdom and of revelation in the knowledge of him, having the eyes of your hearts enlightened, that you may know what is the hope to which he has called you, what are the riches of his glorious inheritance in the saints, and what is the immeasurable greatness of his power toward us who believe*" (Eph. 1:17–19).

It is with your spiritual eyes that you are able to see the things of the Spirit. When others around you see hopelessness and destruction you are able to see beyond the natural to an active, supernatural, and loving God working in you—past, present, and future—that you may rest assured that all is well, though your physical eyes and all your other physical senses tell you differently.

While we can certainly find joy in the glimpses of heaven, those moments of pure heart-pumping happiness, like walking down the aisle with the one we love, or holding our newborn, we may also, through the power of the Holy Spirit, find joy in the *promises* of heaven, those moments when all we can see is a future glory, where we must say with the apostle, *"I consider that the sufferings of this present time are not worth comparing with the glory that is to be revealed to us"* (Rom. 8:18). This means, at times, the only joy you will be able to find is the joy of your salvation. Knowing that you have been undeservedly saved and loved by the God of the universe, and knowing that he has everything under control, might be all that you know of joy, but at least this glimpse of heaven in a sin-darkened world is light enough to show you the way to a joyful life. If all you know is the cross and truth of the gospel, then you have all you need for the Spirit to work in you to grow healthy and abundant fruit.

Joy is found in this knowledge, this unending, unchangeable, unlosable relationship between Father and child, which is yours by the mere fact that we are part of God's family, the temple of the Holy Spirit himself. And because of this fact, because of this Presence, you have within you the capacity to find joy in every moment of your life. Though there may be moments of grief, sorrow, and pain, and those things may be felt to your very core, joy will return in the morning; you will not be overcome. Pain will not be your master or you its slave. When you remember that *"the steadfast love of the* LORD *never ceases; his mercies never come to an end; they are new every morning,"* and you can say, *"The* LORD *is my portion, . . . therefore I will hope in him"* (Lam. 3:22–24), you have found the secret to true joy.

> Let the truth enter deep into us—as long as our joy is not full, it is a sign that we do not yet know our heavenly Vine; every desire for a fuller joy must only urge us to abide more simply and more fully in His love. —Andrew Murray

Consider a mother who loses her child—a horrible nightmare to live through and one of the biggest sources of pain that ever has been. Though complete physical and emotional recovery from such a devastating loss seems unlikely, we are assured that abundant life, promised by Christ, goes on in the soul that is willing to find joy in him. Joy must be available to those of us who suffer, or God is a liar for saying these words to our suffering heart: *"For those who love God all things work together for good, for those who are called according to his purpose"* (Rom. 8:28). Sorrow is a natural result of suffering, but godly sorrow turns to joy when we trust God with all situations, even the terrible ones. Our joy does not betray our pain in those moments but proves its value and gives it purpose. **We must allow him to redeem our pain and make it something important rather than destructive.**

Joy serves a purpose in the life of pain that many have never accurately understood. How beautifully this was seen in life at Ravensbruck. The joy Corrie and Betsie experienced was meant to feed the hungry around them, to shine light in their darkness, to take them away from the power of sin, and to show others the power of a life turned over to the Spirit of God. And while you will likely never live the life these women lived, your life can and will feed the souls of others as the fruit of joy grows in your own life, not for your own pleasure but for the good of the children of God who need some evidence of him in this world.

We make a grave error in thinking that joy exists only for the naturally joyful. For many years I have had a continual sense of joy, of life being just as it should be. But for many years my husband was completely unaware, since, as he pointed out, I had no appearance of joy. What? How can this be? I have always felt so joyful, yet when asked to think of the most joyful people he knew, I wasn't even in the running. This came as a shock to me because I feel so joyful, but after giving it some thought I've come to realize that I was consuming my joy; I was feeling wonderful, content, and happy to be alive, but I wasn't rejoicing outwardly. I wasn't praising God to others or even smiling and laughing. My joy had no witness or witnesses.

I have always believed in honesty, and in honesty I expressed my pain and fatigue so that others could see why I had to collapse on the couch at the end of the day, why I needed a nap in the middle, why my life was too busy to keep the perfect home, and why I didn't have time to play like others do.

My honesty didn't negate my sense of joy; it only trumped it in conversation. To me, joyful people have always seemed fake; after all, how can they act so joyful when life is so hard? How can they speak of joy while suffering and sorrow also exist? My grandmother was called "Sugar," an apt descriptor since she appeared joyful all the time. She never said that anything was wrong; even when others could see differently, she insisted that everything was fine. She never said a negative word, even when one might be needed. When someone was suffering, she acted as if the problem was nothing and literally denied that it was happening. Maybe that's why, for those of us watching, it seemed deceptive, or at the very least ignorant. Life isn't all peaches and cream. There are hard times, there is suffering, pain, and anguish, and to be told that life is great all the time is dishonest. There are many people who try to fool themselves into a blissfully ignorant life and pass it off as joy. The acknowledgment of suffering is not allowed. That kind of joy seemed so fake to me, so the only alternative was brutal emotional honesty.

Since then I have come to see joy in a different light, more like a heartbeat. When you look at the EKG of a healthy heart, you see highs and lows, ups and downs—this consistent sense of falling and rising is the sign of a healthy heart. But if you see an EKG with a flat line, you are looking at a heart that has failed. The person is no longer alive. Joy is something like a beating heart. If it is a flat line, never experiencing the lows of suffering, sorrow, or pain, then it might come across as dead to the world, or at least dead to the realities of pain and suffering. In this scenario the joy is seen as fake, as deceptive and meant only to impress rather than to bring glory to God. And though this may not have been the case with Sugar, it was the impression that it left.

The faux-joyful (or joy-faux!) person can bring disbelief to onlookers, and when that happens, joy becomes more about the tree that grows it than about the lives that witness it. Feelings of joy might serve the purpose of making us feel better, of helping us to avoid reality and suffering, but Spirit-given joy was never meant to remove suffering and sorrow but to complete it. In 1 Peter 1:6–7 we read: *"In this you rejoice, though now for a little while, if necessary, you have been grieved by various trials, so that the tested genuineness of your faith—more precious than gold that perishes though it is tested by fire—may be found to result in praise and glory and honor at the revelation of Jesus Christ."* And Paul writes, *"It has been granted to you that for the sake of Christ you should not only believe in him but also suffer for his sake"* (Phil. 1:29).

We can't be honest in our joy when we are dishonest about our suffering. The fruit of joy feeds those around us not only when life is rosy but also when we can acknowledge that life is difficult and sorrowful. We must find within us the capacity for authentic joy—not joy that ignores failure, sin, and sorrow but joy that rejoices with those who rejoice and weeps with those who weep (see Rom. 12:15). Joy isn't putting on a happy face. **A truly joyful woman sees pain and suffering but also sees the hand of God actively at work and can acknowledge the fleas while thanking God for them.** While joy can come with an amazing feeling of contentment, hope, and delight, it's more than that. Joy can coexist with sorrow and suffering, whereas sorrow without joy is a tyrannical emotion that snuffs out hope and faith. Sorrow, without the underlying truth of God's very nature, without assurance that he is love itself, without a constant reminder of your eternal salvation, will begin to define you and to color all your actions, thoughts, and feelings. Sorrow without joy is a hope stealer, but fruit bearers remember that God is the God of hope (see Rom. 15:13), not of bitterness and doom. With the God of hope living within you, sorrow will remain in check, both experienced and understood as a season, not a destination.

Sorrow isn't meant to be pushed down and ignored (see James 4:9). **It is meant to be a part of all human life, an expression of love lost and of sin felt, but in order for sorrow to be godly, it can't end there. It must find expression in the goodness of God and in the weakness of the sinner.** "*For godly grief produces a repentance that leads to salvation without regret, whereas worldly grief produces death*" (2 Cor. 7:10).

The lack of fruit in our lives doesn't speak to our sad state and our miserable or mediocre life, but to a failure to grasp our purpose here on earth. Many a wise man has said that God's goal isn't to make you happy but to make you holy, yet too often we put our feelings above our faith. We imagine that the fruit of the Spirit was meant to completely satisfy us, but the true purpose of the Spirit's fruit, and therefore your life, isn't happiness but holiness. It is your holiness that indicates that you are being transformed into the image of Christ. As this happens, your abundance overflows as a blessing onto others. As they see the manifestation of the Holy Spirit in your life, they are touched by it, and God is glorified.

So, joy is your purpose, not just your pleasure. It is the fuel to both your service and your contentment. In marriage your joy is a source of your husband's satisfaction and confidence. Your joy speaks volumes to your husband. One of man's most basic desires is to make his wife happy, and when he fails to do that, or when she fails to show it, his life suffers, as does the marriage. A husband is responsible for many things in a marriage, but as this is not a book on the fruitful husband, I will stick to the role of wife and trust that you know I'm not taking sides or asking more of women than I do of men. It is important, however, that as women we work on our own spiritual lives and not those of our husband's, trusting God to do what only God can do best—change man.

That being said, the joyful wife is the *smart* wife. She allows the fruit of the Spirit to nourish not only her husband but also her marriage. She withdraws her criticism, her complaint, and her discontent and finds supernatural cause for joy and delight.

Joylessness

Unfortunately, for many of us, joy is a rare commodity. We have glimpses of it, but certainly not unending days of it. We might even have seasons of complete joylessness. In those moments, the circumstances of life push joy out in favor of more vocal and urgent needs. Joy, then, becomes a luxury, not a necessity, and we find ourselves wondering what evidence we have of the fruit of the Spirit, which is meant to be ours by virtue of our position in Christ. We coast (or scream) through life, accepting our apparent lack of joy as peculiar to our personality type or stage of life, and in so doing we deny the Spirit his working in our lives and instead opt for what can only be considered as sin, for it is a rejection of the direction God has given to "*rejoice always!*" But what sin can be found in our lack of joy? Certainly not sorrow and suffering; those aren't sins but rather the natural and expected result of life on this earth, used by God not to destroy us and starve us of joy but to make our joy complete.

The Joylessness of Doubt

What then is the sin in joylessness? The question is a good one. It can be easy to be content with our lack of joy, but that is dangerous to our souls, because oftentimes it betrays our doubt in the One in whom we claim to believe. Doubt is common amongst believers. We doubt that God will answer our prayers. We doubt that we are worthy of his love and forgiveness. We doubt that we deserve his blessing. Doubt plagues many a woman who has begged God for relief but been given little, if any. But this doubt accuses God of not coming through on his end of the deal and allows you the dark luxury of unbelief.

Doubt about God's ability to forgive, protect, comfort, counsel, or fulfill his promises is a sin and a stealer of joy. Doubt is a fruit of the flesh that cannot conceive of a God as good as ours. But though you can't conceive, you must still believe. It's through the Spirit that you can believe against all odds, find joy against all unbelief, and trust against all doubt that he is who he says he is and that your life is firmly in his hands. Joy comes when you realize that your life is never, for one second, a surprise to God. He hasn't lost all control, and things aren't happening willy-nilly. When you become mindful of the concept of God's complete and total sovereignty in your life, you can find joy in every situation. Doubt steals your joy. But joy is evidence of faith, because joy insists that God is good and that, no matter what the situation, all is well because of him who will never forsake you or leave you (see Josh. 1:5).

The Joylessness of Tired Faith

There is another side of joylessness, one that comes from the misconception that joy is only for the new believer, the child, the inexperienced in the ways of God. Joy can wear off over time, and that reality sets in and leaves little time or need for it. In such cases, the joyless determine that joy isn't a requirement for their faith in God or in their service to him. They mistakenly believe that joy is a bonus, the toy in the Happy Meal, not the main course. But, a lack of joy in the life of a believer demonstrates a lack of appreciation for and love of the One who gave his life so that you may live. A lack of joy also exposes our cavalier attitude toward the wondrous work of Christ on the cross. **If you cannot find reason for joy in either your salvation or God's goodness, then how can others find reason to believe in such a God?**

I preach these words to myself, not because I feel a lack of gratitude but because I fail to express it time and again. Perhaps it's because of my upbringing or personality type that I sense others cannot fully understand my joy and therefore will mock or doubt it. I tend to make my joy a private experience and hoard the fruit all for myself, forgetting that the tree doesn't eat its own fruit but presents it to others. What a fool! Joylessness is my crime, but his blood is my redemption. Thanks be to God!

The Joylessness of Hopelessness

Joylessness betrays our doubt, fear, and even laziness, but it can also betray a more deeply seated sin that can cripple not only the fruit of the Spirit but the very relationship of child to Father, and that is the sin of hopelessness. Hopelessness attacks when things go wrong—when the car breaks down, when the bank repossesses, when the love fades. **Hopelessness**

is a sense that things are not right and never will be again. It is a sense that God has left the building; that he no longer hears our prayers, or, if he does, he just doesn't care to give us what we ask for.

Most of my life I've been a glass-half-empty kind of person. When bad times come I'm not quick to find hope, not quick to look for the silver lining or to see the bright side, and so hopelessness is no stranger to me. This was never so true as when I was pregnant. It was a rough pregnancy and one that had me couch- or bedridden most of the time. I was nauseous all day long, severely bloated, and terribly uncomfortable. Although I knew in my mind that the baby had to come out, I somehow also believed that this was how it would always be, and so I was hopeless. I saw no end to the pain, at least not one that would come soon enough for me, so hopelessness paralyzed me and ultimately made me sicker than I ever needed to be.

I'm one of those women who, when they get a headache that lasts longer than a day, immediately think brain tumor, the eternal pessimist who thinks hope is something for other people who aren't as aware of reality. Assuming the worst is my natural bent, but this pessimistic way discounts the presence of God—active and lovingly involved in my everyday life. Hopelessness assumes he is cruel and detached, toying with our lives like a little boy with a magnifying glass toys with an ant. So I know about hopelessness and its pessimistic spirit. But since I have started to look at the power of the Holy Spirit in the life of those who believe, I've found freedom from hopelessness and the ability to choose hope over pessimism.

The Joylessness of Life on Earth

Many say that they aren't hopeless but, rather, that they have all their hope in heaven. They live for the afterlife, when things will be better, when suffering will cease and wounds will be healed. But a life that hopes only for life after death is a living hell. If your only cause for joy is in leaving this world and going to the next, then, in this world, you have no hope. While joy set before us in the promise of heaven is real and to be trusted, it is not the only joy we have. If you believe it to be your "soul" comfort, your sole source of joy, then you are suffering from joylessness this side of heaven. Joy is for this world as well as the next. "But," you say, "I am joyful. And my thoughts of heaven are the only source of that joy."

Then let me ask, does this joy then feed those around you? Does it bring hope to the hopeless and comfort to the suffering? Does your delight in the things of heaven make life here on earth easier for those who taste of your fruit? Would the joy of death, or the afterlife, have been all the comfort those women in Ravensbruck needed, or was it a joy for this world that was their comfort and strength? Again, your source of joy is in finding the hand of God in your life today and rejoicing in the finished work of Christ. Knowing that your purpose is to serve him and those he loves should bring you joy today.

The Joylessness of Discontentment

A lack of joy in the things that happen this side of heaven speaks to a sin known as discontentment. When nothing that God provides brings you joy, contentment seems a lifetime away. But we all must know that contentment is available for all who believe. And that *"godliness with contentment is great gain"* (1 Tim. 6:6). **Discontentment is being unable to say thank you; it is finding very little in which to hope and nothing in which to rejoice.** For the discontent, for those of us who wish things were different, joy is absent. But we are called to *be content with what we have* (Heb. 13:5), and with this contentment comes the gain of joy for both you and those around you.

CONFESSIONS OF A DISCONTENTED WOMAN. For many years my discontentment stressed me out. I was driven to success, but never quite attained the level I desired. And so I was never content, always wanting more—more money, more stuff, more love. And this discontentment with life led me to busyness, worry, and joylessness. After all, how could I be joyful when I had so much that still needed to be done? But once I took my eyes off of my lack and put them onto his abundance, I found the joy I was lacking. Discontentment no longer robs me of my joy because, through the power of the Spirit, my definition of success has changed. It is now a great success to me to only abide in him, to rest and to trust that where I am is just where he wants me, and in that there is nothing but pure joy.

The Joylessness of a Life Out of Control

Finally, the joyless life can come from a sense that life is out of control. For a lot of us, control is our number-one desire. We covet it, and when we feel it is slipping or has slipped away, we panic, and joy is the furthest thing from our minds. Many women suffer from anorexia, bulimia, and even cutting, all of which most often point to their feeling of being out of control and to their deep desire to regain it. When we have little say over our lives, when others control us or our environment, we can easily lose our sense of joy. But **when we can see the fingerprints of God on our life, when we can trust him with even the badness that comes to us, then we can let go of the need to control our lives.**

The sense that we have our lives under control is, in reality, only an illusion, because God's Word confirms that "*the heart of man plans his way, but the LORD establishes his steps*" (Prov. 16:9). To imagine that if it weren't for so-and-so or such-and-such, life would be different and we would be in control, is deception. *"He does according to his will among the host of heaven and among the inhabitants of the earth; and none can stay his hand or say to him, 'What have you done?'"* (Dan. 4:35). *"Your will be done on earth as it is in heaven,"* is more than a prayer; it's a reality (see Isa. 46:10). As a child of God you must know that all authority in heaven and on earth has been given to Jesus (see Matt. 28:18). And this means that your life is never out of control but under the control of your Savior, the one who died that you might live. This is where your joy is found.

Joy is established in the hope of things unseen rather than in things seen (see 2 Cor. 4:18). When the world around you says all is lost, or even that all is nothing, a boring waste that elicits no chance for excitement or joy, hope says differently. *"But this I call to mind, and therefore I have hope. . . great is your faithfulness"* (Lam. 3:21–23). This hope is the stuff of joy; it has very little to do with circumstances and everything to do with the invisible God, whose hand is actively and lovingly guiding your life not only for his own glory but for your good as well. Your joy can be found in this promise, that *"this light momentary affliction is preparing for us an eternal weight of glory beyond all comparison, as we look not to the things that are seen but to the things that are unseen. For the things that are seen are transient, but the things that are unseen are eternal"* (2 Cor. 4:17–18).

The Joyful Wife

The joyful wife is a blessing to her husband and family. She blesses him with a home that is a pleasure to come to, not because of its cleanliness but because in it there is cheerfulness, optimism, playfulness, and delight. In her, he finds a refuge from the joyless world, an oasis to his parched soul. The man who comes home to a joyless wife finds an irritable, downhearted, negative, cranky, half-hearted woman whose focus on her lack removes from him any of the abundance he may have. Joy is a life giver and an abundance maker. Joy is manifested into energy for others and creates spiritual momentum for the joyful as well. Joy is the fuel of a captivating and unshakable woman who refuses to let doubt or hopelessness serve her insatiable appetite for introspection or pessimism.

Be Mindful

If you want "fruit of the Spirit" joy, then you must learn to be mindful of the power of the Holy Spirit within you to change your life. This isn't something that you do out of your own brute strength; you simply start noticing the Holy Spirit working in you as you keep your eyes on him. Through the Holy Spirit, this impossible journey toward joy in the midst of suffering and sorrow becomes an unbreakable reality, and while it is only through the Spirit that this joy is possible, there must be cooperation on the part of the believer.

To sit and wait for joy to arrive without turning your mind to the things of Christ is like expecting the Holy Spirit to take 15 pounds off your body while sitting on the couch eating ice cream. Scripture confirms the cooperation of the believer in the process of bearing fruit. As we read in James 1:2–4, "*Count it all joy, my brothers, when you meet trials of various kinds, for you know that the testing of your faith produces steadfastness. And let steadfastness have its full effect, that you may be perfect and complete, lacking in nothing.*" James keeps it simple. Start by counting. Take account of how God has worked, is working, and promises to work in your life. This steadfastness, or perseverance, comes from diligently remembering and choosing joy in the midst of trials and suffering. It comes from keeping the faith with a foundation built on God's Word rather than resorting to sin as an escape hatch or defense mechanism.

Choose Optimism

The Holy Spirit is never pessimistic. So as we listen to his voice, as we heed his direction, our lives become optimistic in outlook. As the Spirit of God informs our hearts and minds, we learn to not call conspiracy all that others call conspiracy, and not to fear what others fear, or to dread the future (see Isa. 8:12). When the news demands fear or worry, as in Isaiah's time, the joyful wife refuses to capitulate. When the end is near, the woman who keeps her eyes on Christ sees hope in the destruction rather than gloom or doubt. When the fire ravages or the water floods, she imagines the hand of God setting up opportunities to see his perfect will come to pass and to bring her to a joyful place of rest in his love. **In every circumstance she finds joy, because in everything there is found the hand of God reaching out to the world around her, orchestrating and caring for even the smallest of details in order that his child may bring him glory and find joy everlasting.**

Smile

Not long after my husband pointed out my lack of external joy, I had a conversation with a wonderful friend whose spirit is always light and joyful. We were talking about getting together one day and the busyness of our schedules when she said something life altering: "I have a lot to do this week, and I want to be careful not to lose my smile. So let me look at my schedule and get back to you." **"I want to be careful not to lose my smile"**—those words rang in my head for days. Never before had I heard it put that way, and never before had I seen a woman so devoted to her family that she desired they see her smile every day of her life. This idea sank in, and my face began to change. While I felt it was honest to show my exasperation and fatigue, I started to see the benefit of maintaining a smile over a frown, of having a genuinely joyful face over a sullen or tired one, and I set out to change immediately.

This wasn't putting on a happy face, but maintaining a mindfulness of all that God has done. From that point on, I started to smile when my eyes met the faces of those I loved. I smiled not because of how I felt about my life but because of the life of Christ in me. I smiled a smile of joy, of contentment, of trust. Even when outside forces told me I should be sullen or sad, I still found a reason to smile. I gave honor to my God and to his goodness in something as simple as the movement of my face, and from that came seeds of joy, planted in the lives of those around me. Their faces, in turn, began to lighten, and their concern over my frustration, fatigue, or melancholy left. Joy increased in our household, as the fruit of the Spirit fed those around me, just as it was meant to do.

The very thought of the Holy Spirit should bring a smile to your face. Because of him we can always find reason to offer joy to those around us (see 1 Thess. 5:16). We don't have to paint on a smile, pretending happiness while sadness digs at our soul, but we should consider the benefit of a smile when we look at those whom God has given us for our pleasure and our purpose on earth. Because of him and in him we can find the strength, if for nothing else, to use our facial muscles to say, "*It is well with my soul. 'Though the earth gives way, though the mountains be moved into the heart of the sea, though its waters roar and foam, though the mountains tremble at its swelling,' I will not fear*" (Ps. 46:2–3). And I will not frown.

Encourage One Another

The joyful wife is of great benefit to her husband, from lighting up his home through her cheerfulness and playfulness to offering encouragement and contentment. Her presence isn't a joy sucker but a joy giver. The truth is that we all want to make our mates happy, or at least we did at one time. Even if we don't right now, things can change. Affection that is lost can return, and new, good memories can trump the bad ones. Your marriage can be redeemed no matter how badly you've messed up. It all begins as your love is expressed in joy. This joy, then, can be seen in the way you communicate with your husband. The Fruitful Wife is encouraging, choosing to approve of her husband rather than to disapprove. When a woman disapproves of her man and tells him as much, she is creating more of a problem, because her disapproval may only breed his contempt, laziness, and anger, whereas encouraging words, her approval of him as a man, builds him up and gives him strength.

In 1 Thessalonians 5:11 we are told to *"encourage one another and build one another up."* This isn't just a matter of being a good wife but of being a faithful believer who trusts God with her relationships. So, when it would be easy to criticize or to find fault, the Fruitful Wife opts for joy.

Play

The Fruitful Wife may take her smile to a whole new level by being playful with her husband. One of man's greatest desires is to find in his wife a playmate, someone with whom to joke around and play games and enjoy the simple things of life. Playfulness reveals the joy of your heart in your actions and your words. In nature, animals only play with each other when they feel safe. Just so, your playfulness communicates that you feel safe. Play can express a childlike confidence in the Father, in his ability to manage our affairs, so much so that we can take a break and simply bask in the joys of life and in his companionship. Consider the actions of Mary as she sat at Jesus's feet, as compared to Martha, who served in resentment and bitterness. When you are playful, you allow the fruit of joy to grow plump and juicy and to offer spiritual nourishment to your husband and everyone else who looks on.

Pray

Another amplifier of joy is prayer, and prayer not just for yourself and your need for fruit, but also for those you love. In order to find joy in your marriage, you must pray for your husband. The most powerful words I've ever read on prayer came from a sermon by Charles Spurgeon. He was teaching on the prayer of intercession, of praying for others, and he spoke these words from Job: "*The LORD restored the fortunes of Job, when he had prayed for his friends*" (42:10). Here we see the connection between intercession and blessing. We don't pray in order to be blessed, but God in his graciousness blesses those who selflessly pray for others. And the Fruitful Wife finds a life of abundant joy as she prays day in and day out for her husband, a prayer not of correction and insult, which can be easy when he frustrates, but of blessing and wisdom, of joy and peace. As she prays for her man, so she sees the fruit in her own life. Spirit-given joy will lead to prayer for others, so, as you walk by the Spirit and joy increases, pray more for your man, for yourself, and for your marriage.

* * *

Joy is not out of your reach. It is not reliant on circumstances but on faithfulness, both yours and your God's. When the terrible earthquake of 2010 hit Haiti, a woman found herself trapped under the rubble of her home for four days with no food or water, no comfort, no certainty of rescue. At first she couldn't move. Her arms and legs were trapped, but hour by hour she prayed, she worshiped, and she trusted. Eventually, she began to sense a change. At first she could move her right arm, and then she could move her left leg. As the days went on, she found that she could move her left arm and then her right leg. It was only a small movement, but at least she could get some circulation to her body. When her rescuers saved her, she recounted the words she had said to God as she waited for release. She had prayed, "Thank you for the possibilities, Lord. Thank you for the possibility of movement and for the possibility of rescue." **The joyful wife thanks God for the possibilities.** That might be all there is in her present life—possibilities—but if that's all there is, she can still find joy. She can still worship. She can still pray, and she can still rest in the knowledge that her God has not forsaken her.

But the fruit of the Spirit is
PEACE

3 PEACE

*Peace does not dwell in outward things, but within
the soul; we may preserve it in the midst of the
bitterest pain, if our will remains firm and sub-
missive. Peace in this life springs from acquiescence to, not in an exemption from, suffering.*

—FRANÇOIS FÉNELON

*The Holy Spirit acts as a lubricant to reduce
the friction to a minimum and to stop the fretting and chafing in their grosser phases.*

—A. W. TOZER

Michael and I were married on the beautiful beaches of
Nassau in the Bahamas—the picture-perfect wedding. We
had the beach all to ourselves. The sun was setting behind
us, and the atmosphere was electric. We were both nervous,
for sure; exhausted, no doubt; and anxious about the evening
ahead. Michael had spent the day combing the island for the
perfect wedding location, while I had rested on the beach with
my parents. He had put so much effort into this day. He had
booked the flight, found the hotel, worked the upgrades, and
gotten us a suite on the top floor of the Hilton Hotel. It was
all perfect, or at least it could have been, if it weren't for my
lack of peace. Unfortunately, I had an internal conflict going
on that was monumental. I had waited so long to get married,
some might say out of a fear of commitment, but I say out of
not finding my man until late in life; both might be right. But
still that sense of worry and anxiety over my soon-to-change
life overwhelmed me.

To make matters worse, when they showed us to our room, I was forlorn. It was a nice enough suite, but one glaring problem stressed me and told me this was going to be a bad day: the room didn't have an ocean view but a view of the McDonald's parking lot. *How could this happen?* I thought. *We came to the Bahamas for the ocean, not the fries! Everything was supposed to be perfect.* It almost was until I didn't see tranquil sandy beaches, and then the struggle began. I struggled to be content, joyful, and loving. I struggled for peace and everything that goes with it. And I lost. I spent the next six hours in a state of doubt, worry, and nausea. I had the typical wedding-day jitters along with a dash of resentment, discontentment, and fear. Oh, the joy! Oh, the sin, and, oh, the embarrassment of making this confession.

My self-imposed misery didn't stop there but bled into the night as we consummated the marriage with our first big argument, which ended in harsh words and tears. My lack of peace polluted the entire night, leading me to question things, to find problems and point them out, to doubt some more, and in the end to just shut down. I can say with disgusted confidence that I ruined not only our honeymoon but the first year of our life together with the lack of peace I brought into the marriage.

For the most part, peace has never been a part of my life. In fact, it's only within recent years that I can say that I've tasted of its goodness, or, I should say, allowed others to taste of it in my life. My lack of peace has poisoned the lives of countless people and, most importantly, my husband's. Before I understood the reasons for my inner and outer conflicts, before I knew the role I played in both, I assumed *my* peace was the responsibility of others, especially those others who loved me. If I lacked peace it was because they weren't supplying what was required. The right environment was essential for my peace, and without that I was in continual conflict.

And so I walked out on every relationship and situation that I felt lacked peace, as if I wasn't the ultimate cause but only an innocent bystander. I, in essence, blamed my sin on others. So, it is a great surprise that I didn't walk away from Michael that first year. I am certain I would have if it weren't for my mindfulness of God's disdain for divorce outside of the presence of adultery or abandonment. So certain I was of this command not to separate what he has joined together (Mark 10:9) that I didn't dare walk away. And thank God for that, because, through perseverance and faith, I ultimately allowed the Holy Spirit to give me something I had never had before, no matter what the circumstances or relationship: peace in the midst of the unknown.

I, like countless others, was under this debilitating impression that peace, both inner and outer, was ultimately for my own good, and so my lack of it didn't hurt anyone but me. I was oblivious to the fact that my fruit, the fruit I figured was optional in the life of faith, was instead meant to glorify God and nourish those around me, leading them to its true source. I took no responsibility for being a peacemaker (Matt. 5:9), and I didn't consider my internal lack of peace as a contradiction to Romans 14:19, which says, "*So then let us pursue what makes for peace and for mutual upbuilding.*"

But I'm glad to say that now things are completely different. I have tasted the secret to peace in any and all situations. I have discovered the source of contentment that Paul talks about in Philippians 4:11–13: "*I have learned in whatever situation I am to be content. I know how to be brought low, and I know how to abound. In any and every circumstance, I have learned the secret of facing plenty and hunger, abundance and need. I can do all things through him who strengthens me.*" But this wasn't an easy journey; it was filled with struggle, strife, and failure, as it is even now. It takes the attention of all my heart, soul, mind, and strength as well as an understanding not only of peace but of the opposite of peace and the ways I allowed it into my life.

What Is Peace?

For most of the world, peace, like happiness, has to do with circumstances. The absence of strife, struggle, antagonism, and war means the presence of peace. Many believe that they can have no peace until there is an absence of suffering and irritation in their life. How many women have exclaimed, "Can I just get a little peace around here!" in response to the continual interruptions and demands made on her by those she loves? We all feel it, that nagging sense that peace is not available in our busy, hectic, and demanding lives. But the "fruit of the Spirit" peace, the kind of peace that survives the most unpleasant of circumstances, was never meant to be reliant on anything or anyone other than the Spirit for its presence. That means that even if war rages around you, peace can be yours. And this is good news. It means **you don't have to completely reengineer your life in order to find peace today.**

Peace comes from an absence of conflict, not external conflict but internal conflict. Though war rages externally, there still can be peace within. **Peace in this life comes from your acceptance of suffering, not your exemption from it.** Such acceptance is peace, and it carries with it freedom from the worry that naturally attends difficult, frightening, or dangerous situations. It is a calm knowing and a restful understanding of the ways of a world held in the hand of a perfect God.

In 1956 Elisabeth Elliot heard the horrifying news that her husband Jim and four other men had been killed while attempting to bring the message of the gospel to the Auca Indians in Ecuador. These missionaries were killed by the very people they had gone to serve. Elizabeth grieved. She had loved Jim with all her heart; but that wasn't the end of the story for Elizabeth as she and her young daughter, Valerie, returned to the people who had taken the second-most-important man in their lives to minister to them and to continue the work of teaching them about the saving love of Jesus Christ. When asked how she could summon the courage to return to such a terrible place under such horrific conditions, she responded with words that should give us all a reason to believe peace is possible, even in our most tiresome of trials. She said, "The growth of all living green things wonderfully represents the process of receiving and relinquishing, gaining and losing, living and dying. . . . The truth is that it is ours to thank Him for and ours to offer back to Him, ours to relinquish, ours to lose, ours to let go of—if we want to find our true selves, if we want real life, if our hearts are set on glory."[4] These are powerful words from a woman who had just suffered the loss of her husband, the father of her child. But consider this, that if this woman can respond with such peace in the face of such loss and sorrow, then that means peace isn't dependent on circumstances at all. If anyone had cause for the battles of worry, anger, and bitterness, Elisabeth Elliot did, yet peace was hers in the midst of it all, and peace can be yours in the midst of the struggles of your life.

The Fruit of Peace

In John 14:27, Jesus made this promise to the chaotic, busy, and worried world: *"Peace I leave with you; my peace I give to you. Not as the world gives do I give to you. Let not your hearts be troubled, neither let them be afraid."* So how come this peace isn't ours from sunrise to sunset and sunset to sunrise? How come we struggle, fight, and worry our way through life? Why doesn't the fruit of peace grow as plentifully as it could? Maybe a way to answer this question would be to look at the life of fruit. If you want to grow an abundant crop of oranges in your backyard, you first have to plant an orange tree. You wouldn't plant a palm tree and expect it to give you oranges. And the same law applies to the fruit of peace. In order to have the peace *of* God in your life and in your relationships, you must first have the tree from which that peace grows, and that is found in peace *with* God.

Peace with God

The tranquility of mind that comes from having a right relationship with God is the source of all our peace. And when we have that peace, as it says in Psalm 119:165, nothing can make us stumble. We can be certain of this peace with God because of what we read in Romans 5:1: "*Since we have been justified by faith, we have peace with God through our Lord Jesus Christ.*" Jesus's blood is our ransom from sin's punishment, and it not only purchased our *peace with God* but also gives us access to the *peace of God* that passes all understanding (Phil. 4:7). It is this foundational *peace with God* that plows the way for the *peace of God* and ultimately the *peace with our fellow man.*

It's a natural human tendency to think that peace is situational, dependent on our circumstances and the people around us. Believe me, I have gone after this source of peace most ravenously. In fact, it's the one I demand in order to be productive, happy, calm, and sometimes even kind. There is nothing more refreshing than a clean house. Right after I get everything dusted, mopped, and put in its rightful place, peace engulfs me like a big feather bed with Egyptian cotton sheets. The mess that often surrounds me makes me miserable, short-tempered, and overwhelmed, so the days of neat and clean that I get are an oasis in a desert of disorder. But this kind of peace is so fleeting, so hard to manufacture, and so demanding of my time and energy. I feel as if I'm in a continual battle for victory over disorder.

For many of us, if pressed, we would probably admit that our sense of peace is situational, grounded in surroundings, feelings, and relationships. For much of our marriage Michael and I had little peace. Conflict was our average fare. My ways rubbed him wrong and, since my peace was born in situation and he was a major part of my situation, when he challenged or corrected me I fought back, and the battle was on. This situational, or relational, source of peace that we manufactured was faulty at best, as is any kind of peace based on anything or anyone other than the Unchanging One. But our relationship with each other improved when our relationship with the Holy Spirit became not a coincidental part of our peace but the sole source of it. We both had peace with God as we came into our Christian marriage, but it all stopped there because we had failed to grab hold of the *peace of God*.

An understanding of the peace of God that is available to all who believe is crucial for peace with man. So let's take a quick look at this peace of God and what it means. **The peace of God allows for peace from guilt.** I could restate the following in more modern vernacular, but to do so sounds less than inspirational, and so I'll leave these words of Thomas à Kempis intact: "Thou wilt enjoy tranquility if thy heart condemn thee not." Peace comes when guilt is forgiven, and forgiveness is given to all who freely confess their sins (Ps. 32:5).

The peace of God also provides peace from striving. Striving is something we all tend to do. We all know what we want, and it takes work to get it, so we strive for it, even in our spiritual lives. We work hard for what we want with self-determination, planning, and scheming. But the peace of God removes that requirement from our lives. This is what Jesus was talking about when he said, "*Come to me, all who labor and are heavy laden, and I will give you rest. Take my yoke upon you, and learn from me, for I am gentle and lowly in heart, and you will find rest for your souls. For my yoke is easy, and my burden is light*" (Matt. 11:28–30). The rest he offers is a release from the burden of striving. A. W. Tozer explains rest this way: "It is not something we do, it is what comes to us when we cease to do. His own meekness, that is the rest."[5] And so it is with peace. Peace comes when you stop striving and rely on the Holy Spirit to do for you.

The peace of God also allows for peace from pretending. There is a time in all of our lives when we pretend we are something that we are not in order that we might impress, succeed, or survive. But pretending breeds unrest, inner conflict, and doubt. When we pretend to be something we are not, deep down inside we struggle and suffer over what the pretend us hides about the true us, and peace is out of our grasp. The peace of God comes not from who we are, but in who he is and what he has done for us. "*God is not a God of confusion but of peace*" (1 Cor. 14:33), and so from him comes clarity and peace in our position as children of God. The peace of God not only allows us to be ourselves; it proves the value of transparency, honesty, and confession (James 5:16). When we are real about who we are—our shortcomings, blunders, and sins—we arrive at peace through the healing of community.

And finally, **the peace of God provides peace from worry and fear.** Worry and fear have to do with future events, the unknown, expected disaster or failure, loss or suffering. The peace of God removes any uncertainty about your "fate," your future, and even your eternity. Knowing that God is an active, loving, and all-powerful Father who doesn't allow anything in your life except what is for your ultimate good (Rom. 8:28; 1 Cor. 12:18; Eph. 1:11) removes the need for worry and fear. Only those who *don't* believe in a sovereign God working actively in their lives feel a need for worry and fear in order to manage and control their own destiny. And this job is filled with strife. Peace is available to all who have not only heard what God has said but also believed it.

So, the "fruit of the Spirit" peace finds its origin in peace with God and its freedom in the peace of God, and it is evidenced in peace with man. There can be peace with man without peace with God, but the kind of peace we are talking about is beyond the grasp of anyone who hasn't been indwelt by the Holy Spirit. Peace may come for awhile to the unbelieving, but when the fire burns too hot, their peace is soon replaced with terror, struggle, and worry. It is foundational peace with God that gives us access to the peace of God that guards our hearts and minds, rules in our lives, and ultimately makes us one body (Phil. 4:7; Col. 3:15). This kind of peace has a rich texture that perfectly allows for complete freedom from the internal conflict that the rest of the world struggles with. And that is why it passes all understanding; it is supernatural in origin. It is the peace of harmony and unity that we read of in Acts 4:32, where it says that the believers in the early church *"were of one heart and soul."* They were described this way only after they had been given the Holy Spirit. It is only in union with Christ that we are able to live in peace.

God's Call for Peace

In Psalm 34:14 we are told to *"seek peace and pursue it"* because love requires it. Fights, arguments, dissension, and rebellion are not aspects of love but of sin. We read about these "works of the flesh" in Galatians 5:19–21. Love shows itself in the presence of peace, so that even if others should rage in anger or hatred, love compels us not to join in the insanity. Peace enables us to remain in the calmness of faith in the One who is greater than all the drama. Your peace speaks to your love for God and for others. **It is hard to see the love in war, in screams and shouts, attacks and insults, and so God commands a peace that trumps our desire to be heard, to stand up for ourselves, or to win.**

James 3:18 teaches that *"a harvest of righteousness is sown in peace by those who make peace."* The righteousness that we all desire finds its root in the peace that we make.

Have you ever considered that God is the God of peace (Rom. 15:33), Jesus is the Prince of Peace (Isa. 9:6), and that you have embraced the gospel of peace (Rom. 10:15 NKJV)? Your peace, then, is a part of your faith in the God of peace. In fact, peace is the evidence of your trust in him. When there is a lack of peace, when your heart worries, frets, fights, or fears, and peace is absent, your lack of peace calls God a liar. A lack of peace points to doubt in God's goodness, compassion, mercy, and love. And while you might never say the words "I don't trust God," your lack of peace says it without words. **Peace is the living out of faith and, conversely, conflict is the living out of doubt and distrust in the God of peace.**

The call for peace is for your good. It isn't an indictment on your inability to relax and let things go, but a prescription for your health. God knows that a heart of unrest, worry, and conflict is bad for you. In Proverbs 12:25 he says that *"anxiety in a man's heart weighs him down."* And in Luke 21:34 he blames our anxiety over the cares of this life for our heavy hearts. Peace is meant to bring your body to health. If there is a heaviness to your heart, a wasting away of your body, a failure of strength, it just might point to your lack of peace, in the area of relationship either to God or to his creation. **God's call for peace is for both the good of the corporate body as well as the physical one.** From Jesus we learn that *"if a house is divided against itself, that house will not be able to stand"* (Mark 3:25), and nothing divides a house more than a lack of peace. So God's call for peace is essential to the life of faith and the fellowship with both God and man.

Peace Thieves

Unfortunately, if you ask most women if their lives are peaceful, chances are you are going to hear no. Conflict, struggle, worry, disorder, chaos, stress, noise, regret, resentment, discontentment, and bitterness color our lives on a daily basis.

Peace is something occasionally found in thirty minutes at the spa, or fifteen minutes with a cup of coffee and an empty house, but not something available in the normal hectic pace of daily life, we reason. And with that reasoning comes an unspoken resignation to a life with only small glimpses of tranquility in "me time" rather than a lifestyle of peace and quietness of heart.

So what has stolen the peace that Jesus left with us all? Who or what is the thief that has stolen the very precious commodity of supernatural peace from our lives? The Bible lists several areas where peace is vulnerable and where we let go of it in favor of holding on to something else. In Matthew 6 Jesus talks about the peace thief of self-protection, that part of us that is looking out for our good and so frets away with the intent to protect us from the disaster of not having enough to eat or to wear. Anxiety over these things robs you of peace. When you worry about your wardrobe, or lack thereof, when you fret over food, worshiping it through either overindulging or withholding, you lose the peace that was meant to be yours. But, instead, when you trust the Prince of Peace and *"seek first the kingdom of God and his righteousness . . . all these things will be added to you"* (Matt. 6:33). So **self-protection is the first peace thief we encounter.**

This self-protective muscle is seen not only in our personal life but also in our relationships. It shows up in what the Bible calls "rivalries" (Gal. 5:20), which covers things like competition, contention, conflict, friction, and fighting. **This sense of rivalry, or self-interest, steals the peace from both your life and the life of the one you feel compelled to beat.** Standing up for ourselves promises safety and benefit, but what it brings is unrest, conflict, and dissension.

In my life, rivalry has been the norm. When anyone disagrees with me, even in the area of faith, my tendency is to argue, to prove my point, to be victorious. I don't like to lose, and I especially don't want to be proven wrong. So my first instinct is contention. So certain am I of my perfection, my wisdom, and my rightness that I quickly battle any dissenter or agitator against my "divine" reason. So the story goes, and so the mess is made. My prideful sense of being the "rightest" has stolen days, if not years, of peace from my life. In this area of competition for supremacy I have had to administer the following verse: *"For where jealousy and selfish ambition exist, there will be disorder and every vile practice. But the wisdom from above is first pure, then peaceable, gentle, open to reason, full of mercy and good fruits, impartial and sincere"* (James 3:16–17). What a challenge—to be open and impartial to reason when their reason is so different from mine, and impartial when I like my ideas the best! But the peace of God demands it. **When we let our self-protection dominate our relationships, we open the door to the treasury of peace and invite the thieves in.**

At the root of all this lack of peace is the single-most-destructive thought in the life of faith, and that is doubt. Faith, by definition, is believing, not doubting. How easy it is for us to coddle our doubts, to make excuses for them and to raise our hands in complete surrender to our lack of ability to trust our God. Doubt is a peace thief; it steals the peace of God from our lives. To your doubt Jesus applies this balm: *"Let not your hearts be troubled. Believe in God; believe also in me"* (John 14:1). **The heart that is troubled is the heart that doesn't believe. But faith restores peace.**

Much of our peace in this life is stolen by our failure to find comfort in God. Where you go for comfort in the midst of trouble determines the amount of peace you will find. In John 16:30, Jesus promises us a peace found in his mastery of this troubled world, yet so often we look for a more tangible release from trials and tribulations. As women, we tend to search for it in the beauty we possess, either in ourselves or in our closets, or in food, success, romance, love, or even pain. And self-injury is a go-to comforter for some of us who have found no relief in any other part of life. Unfortunately, all of these "homemade" remedies come with a dangerous side effect, and that is a complete and total lack of peace.

For years I was an advocate of shopping therapy. At the end of a bad day, the only thing that soothed me as much as a gallon of ice cream and a spoon was going shopping and buying stuff. Over time I racked up thousands of dollars of debt. So strong was my desire for stuff I couldn't afford that the outcome of all that "therapy" was financial hardship that came from $20,000 of credit card debt. As a single girl trying to pay all the bills myself, this was overwhelming—so overwhelming that my worry gave way to stomach pains, gut issues, back problems, and headaches. What I longed for in the acquisition of stuff ended up stealing from me the very thing it promised.

When we think that stuff—anything other than God—will be our salvation or comfort, we fall prey to another thief of peace, idolatry. How easy it is to see stuff and to find pleasure in it, then to want more and more of it in order to get more and more pleasure. This is the very process by which idols are made. An idol is stuff we go to for the things that God promises to do for us, and peace is one of those things. So the biggest peace thief of all is looking for peace in all the wrong places.

Living in Perfect Peace

Living in relationship with other human beings, especially with those who are so much different from us, can be challenging to our peace. Human interaction requires a lot of energy, participation, and thought, all of which can get in the way of peace. When people disagree with you and your decisions, when you are too busy to deal with their questions, when they fail you or reject you, when you are worried, uncomfortable, or afraid, peace can seem impossible. Can the peace of the Spirit still grow in your life when conditions are unfavorable? According to 2 Thessalonians 3:16 peace is available in every situation. Paul ends the letter with these words: *"Now may the Lord of peace himself give you peace at all times in every way."* Paul would not have prayed these words had they not been possible.

Surrender to the Vine

But how do you prepare the soil for success? How do you encourage "fruit of the Spirit" peace to grow in your life? And what role do you play, if any, in its manifestation? As in all aspects of faith, it is God who grants it. We have our faith to the measure *"that God has assigned"* (Rom. 12:3), and it grows as we abide in Christ, the vine (John 15:5). So faith isn't something that has to be struggled to gain or worked at, but accepted with open arms. This open-arm position speaks to the surrender that is required in order for faith to do its work. **There must be complete surrender to the Holy Spirit, to the vine, in order for the fruit to grow.** The Holy Spirit is the sap that runs through your branches and feeds the fruit of peace in your life. And while desiring the fruit of the Spirit is a good thing, fretting over the lack of it, or being plagued by your inability to produce it, is self-destructive and unsurrendered. Let Christ, the vine, bear the responsibility of fruit. And don't spoil the very fruit of peace that you crave by weighing your-self down with the cares of the vine.

Set Your Mind on the Spirit

It is your part simply to set your mind on the Spirit, not to take over for the Spirit. It is in the mind where the choice is made, the choice between the things of this world and the things of the Spirit. In Romans 8:6 we are told that *"to set the mind on the flesh is death, but to set the mind on the Spirit is life and peace."* So your mind must be set on the things above, and you do this by keeping the Word of God ever running through your mind.

A while ago I started the experiment of memorizing large chunks of Scripture. I started taking the Psalms and turning them into songs. As I sang the songs over and over again, I found that memorization came quickly, and so did my sense of peace. The bathing of one's self in God's Word has a peaceful effect. And as you read it and memorize it, you are setting your mind on the Spirit. As you begin to reorient your thoughts onto these more important things, the previously "important" stuff of life fades into the background, and so does all the noise that attended it.

Be Willing to Lose

After your mind has been set on the things of God, your thoughts fall into line, and when this happens your heart softens to the things that used to chafe and scratch. In relationship to man, then, this becomes the secret to peace. And this is how it plays out. **The mind set on the things of the Spirit becomes willing to lose.** Most of our struggle and strife in relationship to others comes from our severe distaste for losing. When winning takes a back seat to peace, things begin to change. In contradiction to our very human nature Jesus says, *"The last will be first, and the first last"* (Matt. 20:16). Winning's reward in heaven is loss, and the reward for loss is a win. Knowing this allows the mind, set on the things above, to be willing to lose and, in fact, to find no real satisfaction in the win itself. In the battle that often rages between men and women, this idea is fertile ground for peace.

WILLING TO LOSE. In my marriage, I used to be certain that not only did I have to win; I had to be understood and heard. Because of that, our arguments were long and drawn out. But once I gave up my need to win, I discovered peace was more quickly restored to our relationship. For a lot of women this might sound like complete folly, giving up being right. But in the economy of God this is not folly but faith. In keeping with his mathematics, God shows us that it's not the victor or the strong—not the fittest, as Darwin would have us believe—but the loser, those who have abdicated winning in the competition of life for victory in Jesus, who wins.

Be Willing to Be Ignored

The Holy Spirit's voice is one of peace, and as we begin to respond to that voice we find a willingness to be ignored, misunderstood, and even rejected in our relationships without sinning. The Holy Spirit has no need for positioning, for argument, or for attention seeking, and it doesn't insist on being heard. And so the lover of the Spirit is able, along with Christ, to entrust herself to him who judges justly, just as Christ did when people hurled insults at him and threatened and accused him (1 Pet. 2:22–23). He did not fight for himself but rested in the peace of God, knowing that God had the final say.

Don't Be Easily Offended

We do not practice peace when we allow the sins of others to offend us, to lead us to the sin of resentment, bitterness, or any other emotion that conflicts with peace and faith in the God who takes care of everything. As we read in Proverbs 19:11, *"Good sense makes one slow to anger, and it is his glory to overlook an offense."* The willingness to overlook an offense comes more easily to the woman who has her heart set on bringing God the glory and showing little concern for her own. And in this, the woman animated by the Spirit finds herself supernaturally getting over her right to get even, to teach him a lesson, or to exact revenge: *"Beloved, never avenge yourselves, but leave it to the wrath of God, for it is written, 'Vengeance is mine, I will repay, says the Lord.' To the contrary, 'if your enemy is hungry, feed him; if he is thirsty, give him something to drink; for by so doing you will heap burning coals on his head.' Do not be overcome by evil, but overcome evil with good"* (Rom. 12:19–21).

Forgive the Offender

As the Holy Spirit gives us the "fruit of the Spirit" peace, he enables us to forgive those who offend us. Following the act of confession and repentance is forgiveness. And while God doesn't give us the ability to completely forget the offense, a continual abiding in Christ does enable us not to bring it up again as leverage in future disputes. As we listen to the voice of God over self, we start to release our need to obsess over the wrong done by others, because we are more aware of the wrong done by ourselves and the forgiveness given to us by God.

✳ ✳ ✳

"You keep him in perfect peace whose mind is stayed on you, because he trusts in you" (Isa. 26:3). Perfect peace! Can you imagine having that in your life? Well, you can have it, and you can have it today. If you've failed up until now, don't let that be cause for more worry and regret. Peace grows from a branch connected to the vine. For a long time I believed that the fruit was my responsibility, and I carried guilt that the fruit wasn't more evident in my life. True peace is mine by way of the vine, that is, Christ, whose Spirit lives in me and animates me so that I may daily become more and more like him. If what you are feeling, thinking, or doing seems to

separate you from the very vine that is meant to sustain you, then you must remind yourself of who God is and what he's done and return to abide in the vine. Peace will be yours when you acquire it this way, not when you strive for it all alone. Peace comes when you abandon yourself to the Prince of Peace and accept the peace of God that passes all understanding. Surrender not to the chaos and strife of this world, but to the God of peace, who is the only answer to a life of beautiful and permanent peace.

But the fruit of the Spirit is
PATIENCE

4 PATIENCE

*If suffering is completely in God's hands, why don't
we just leave it up to his will? Why don't we believe
that, just as he can bring us back to a trial when we run
away, he can also protect us when we don't run away?*

—TERTULLIAN

*You may often see Jesus Christ wreck
a life before He saves it.*

—OSWALD CHAMBERS

I'm prone to impatience. When I want my computer to do
something and it doesn't do it immediately, I begin banging
on the keyboard to convince it of my urgency. When others
drive slowly in front of me, I want to scream, and when my
daughter won't put her shoes on after I've asked her more than
five times, I want to throw the shoes across the room. When
people don't do what I want, when they get in my way or slow
me down, I lose it. So practiced am I in the art of speed and
getting things done that impatience has become my first reaction. I can feel the adrenal rush to my brain; my heart starts to
feel like it will explode if I can't change the situation fast. My
ways are, in my estimation, far better than the ways of every
other person around me, and a quick acquiescence to that fact
would save us all a lot of grief in the end, or so I reason.

Most of my life I figured that patience was reserved for
only the few souls born with it. Schoolteachers, health care
givers, missionaries—I've seen many gifted with patience,
sailing through life as if working with difficult people didn't
bring on a torrent of ugly emotions. But putting up with delay,

suffering pain without complaint, and trusting God with my time and energy do not come naturally to me, and so patience has not been a fruit found growing on my spiritual tree. This, however, became unacceptable to me when I started to think about the fruit of the Spirit as nourishment for others and not for myself. For me, I could exist just fine if my impatience could persuade the rest of the world to get into line with my ideas of what needs to be done and when. I'd be just fine taking the matters of life into my own hands and "gettin' 'er done." Until I got married, I was able to hide most of my impatience from prying eyes. But once I had a husband observing my craving for immediate action, my constant frustration with the speed of my computer, and the inability of everyone else to do things when I wanted them done, I started to see the insanity of a life without the fruit of patience in it.

I was so used to planning my life and working out its details that, even when I decided to share my life with another, I kept on living as if I were still in charge. When my new partner failed to do exactly what my plans demanded, I would do it for him—clean up his messes, fix his "errors," redo his work. We've heard that when a couple is in love, they can complete each other's sentences. Well, I would complete Michael's sentences, not because we were so close but because I was too impatient to wait for him to finish. So perfect was my knowledge and wisdom that anyone else, including the man I married, could not begin to keep up with me, or so I thought in my impatience and sin.

What Is Patience?

Patience is more than the ability to wait. It involves a capacity to resist the temptation to play God, not only in your own life but in the lives of others as well. Patience looks at difficult people not as an imposition but as a part of the tapestry of a life woven by God himself. **Patience tolerates delay because it**

sees the hand of God in every event, and patience can suffer pain without complaint because to complain is to accuse God of some wrongdoing. Patience lives out of a love for God and for man that trumps the love of schedule, plans, or expectations. Patience trusts God to such an extent that nothing, not even the most heinous interruption, can lead to frustration, resentment, or explosion.

Impatience essentially speaks to the distaste we all have for interruptions to our comfort. We are comfortable with our own ways of doing things, our own pace, our own plans; and when there is an interruption or a change to those expectations, our patience is tested. And if our patience is a human trait, then its strength will waiver, but if it is a "fruit of the Spirit" trait, then its resolve is sure.

A Patient Look at Impatience

Impatience is the fiber of most our lives, and we don't even realize when it is showing its ugly face. Impatience is at the root of many of our sins. A short temper is sometimes the most obvious, seen in those moments when we are easily angered by the choices, actions, or words of others. Impatience has no time for delay and makes sure everybody knows it. Putting up with the stupidity, error, and obstruction of others is a sign of patience, but the inability to remain kind, calm, and even-tempered when confronted with any of those three diagnoses our impatience.

A big part of impatience is complaint. For me, complaint has always been my way of being honest, of sharing my deepest feelings and of connecting on a deeper level with others, or so I imagined. A complaint voiced and agreed on by another is a sweet thing. It can feel like a bond has been made, like a part of our soul has been shared with another, and because of that a connection is sparked, and so we complain in order to be understood and known. Complaints demand to be spoken.

How hard it is to hold them in and to refuse to release the frustration that accompanies them. But to complain is to voice our impatience. **Complaint, most often, expresses the inability to endure suffering** (2 Tim. 4:5), even of the most inconsequential kind. And when complaint seems most warranted, as in the case of unfair imprisonment or torture, patience bears with mankind as it sees not chaos and loss but order and hope.

In the early years of my dating life I was so confident in myself and my wisdom that I took control of my love life, asking men out, defining the relationship, taking charge. And when I got married, I continued to imagine that my being in control was best. In that regard, I don't think I'm the exception among modern females. We are assertive, knowledgeable, self-sustaining, and competent, and we don't "need" men or anyone else to take care of us. Many of us are tempted to take control in any and every situation, but attempting to take **control can be a sign of our impatience.** When we see something not being done right or quick enough, taking control is acting upon our impatience. And while things might just get done more efficiently and cleanly, they are done in the strength not of the fruit of the Spirit but of the flesh. And for those of us who fit this category, we must remember that "*to set the mind on the flesh is death, but to set the mind on the Spirit is life and peace*" (Rom. 8:6).

Another symptom of our impatience is boredom. Boredom speaks to our impatience with life. When we are bored, we wish things were moving quicker, and we oftentimes do things in our boredom that celebrate our impatience. It wasn't long ago that I connected my inability to read an entire e-mail to my impatience and boredom. Many a time I have missed some important information or instruction because I was too impatient to read to the end of the e-mail. Anything that seems boring I desperately wish to avoid, even if it is something that I really need to do. In my impatience with doing boring tasks, like reading instructions, I get into all kinds of trouble. But I have to remind myself that patience bears with the boring essentials in order to hear what needs to be heard, or learn what needs to be learned. Patience knows the value of suffering boredom well.

Those who can't suffer boredom well might be, by biblical definition, lazy. When we avoid doing what needs to be done because it seems unappealing or boring, we are being lazy. While you wouldn't often think of a lazy person as an impatient person, because it's a different kind of impatience, notice that the lazy teenager is impatient with the work required of her, and so she avoids it all together rather than patiently put up with her labors. After all, you can easily see that in areas of interest for the teen, laziness isn't an issue. If we want to do something badly enough, the boredom factor is zero and so then is the laziness. We are warned of laziness in Hebrews 6:12: "*We do not want you to become lazy, but to imitate those who through faith and patience inherit what has been promised*" (NIV). So **it is through faith and patience that laziness is averted. Patience keeps us moving forward, no matter how monotonous or boring the journey.**

Impatience is also revealed in our inability to rest in the sovereignty of God. Our inability to find rest keeps us in a constant state of anxiety and stress. Impatience feeds negative emotions by convincing us that where we are isn't where we should be and that what we are doing isn't enough. **Impatience fails to find rest because it mistakenly believes that work is the answer to those feelings of discontent, and when work is not an option, we find ourselves anxious or bored with our condition.** But patience that grows from the presence of the Spirit of God within us lives in such contentment and certainty in the goodness of God that no slowdown, detour, or boredom can remove it. **When the Spirit's agenda supersedes our own, patience comes more easily.**

Unfortunately, for many of us this restlessness finds no relief in the things of the Spirit and soon raises its voice and demands not only movement but rigorous movement, as may be the case of those with obsessive compulsive disorder, hypochondria, or other social phobias. **The kinds of neuroses that are born in our spirits, that find life in our fear, impatience, and doubt in the lovingkindness and goodness of God, would find relief in our spirits should we align ourselves with God the Holy Spirit and allow him to gently produce the fruit of patience in our lives.** It is the obsessive personality that worships something other than God and serves it to the point of illness and refuses to submit that obsession to the One who is meant to be our only obsession. In this we form an "immoderate attachment or devotion to something"[6] other than God, and we thus create for ourselves an idol, which we serve as a little god that promises to protect us or save us from suffering and danger.

People who are nervous or high strung are similarly plagued with their own impatience. Often referred to as type A personalities, of which I am one, these people are driven to impatience by the requirements they put on themselves. The truth is that each of us has an unwritten set of rules about how things *should* be done and how *others* should behave. This unwritten law drives us and governs our energy level and usage.

So as not to beat a dead horse and linger too long on the problem of impatience, let me close all of this talk by saying that there isn't one human being who doesn't at some point struggle with impatience. But the impatience that plagues us, that hurts those we love and leads us to all kind of physical and mental ills, must be addressed. And thankfully, this can be changed by a refocusing of our minds onto the source of all patience, the very Holy Spirit that lives within us. If I haven't been convincing so far, let me say again that I am by nature extremely impatient, and today I can say that through the power of the Holy Spirit, I have been able to find patience I never knew would be possible in my life; the same can be true for everyone who is willing to set their mind on the things above.

Patient Fruit

So now would be a good time to reorient our hearts and minds onto the things of God and off the things of this world. First of all, let me just say that patience isn't reserved for those who are naturally calm, kind, or gracious. It is a calling on the lives of the saints, which includes you if you have put your faith in Christ. Romans 12:12 confirms this call on our lives when it says that as believers we are to *"rejoice in hope, be patient in tribulation, be constant in prayer."* Here we see that hope, patience, and prayer are all a part of the life of faith, an evidence of the life of God in us. That's why we can say with assurance that patience is no more reserved for the few "blessed" ones than prayer is reserved for the few prayerful ones.

We must understand that **patience serves also in the avoidance of sin.** When we reject the possibility of compliance to *any* of God's direction because of our natural disposition, we sin. In that sin we consider God too demanding to be obeyed, and in so doing we call God cruel for seeming to demand the impossible. God, however, asks only things that are possible for us to do and only things that are for our good as well. When we learn patience and see it growing in ourselves through his Spirit, we not only avoid the sin of impatience but many other sins like revenge (Rom. 12:19), bitterness (Heb. 12:15), grumbling (James 5:9), complaining (Phil. 2:14), resentment (1 Cor. 13:5), worry (Matt. 6:25), anxiety (Phil. 4:6), arguments (Titus 3:2), coveting (Mark 7:22), and the like, which spring from impatience. How easy it is to allow impatience to be our reaction when people do bad things, things that beg us to stand up for ourselves, to fight for our rights. But God's Word is clear: we must *patiently endure evil* (see 2 Tim. 2:24–26). To the wife, this means there is no excuse for impatience with her husband but rather the call for a grace-filled and patient response to his mistakes and failings through the power of the Holy Spirit.

Trust me, **one day patience will save your life.** Take a look at these words found in Luke 21:19: *"By your endurance you will gain your lives."* Endurance, or patience in trials and suffering, is good for you, though it might not feel that way at the time. In James 1 we find the benefits of endurance, or steadfastness, when it tells us that our endurance results in our becoming "perfect and complete, lacking in nothing" (vv. 2–4). So patience serves not only others but also ourselves as it perfects us and leaves us wanting for nothing.

Patience is also important for the life we will live after we die. In Romans 2:7 we read that *"to those who by patience in well-doing seek for glory and honor and immortality, he will give eternal life."* And in Hebrews 10:36 we read that *"you have need of endurance, so that when you have done the will of God you may receive what is promised."* Not that your salvation depends on what you do, because it is reliant on what Christ did; but your endurance proves God's will. And as a part of endurance we must practice patience, not only with others but in our own suffering and trials. Patience, as a part of God's very character, is important in the life of his children, those who will inherit his kingdom. Of this patience we read that *"the Lord is not slow to fulfill his promise as some count slowness, but is patient toward you, not wishing that any should perish, but that all should reach repentance"* (2 Pet. 3:9). So our patience is an imitation of God, who has had more than enough patience with his children. Yet we lash out in frustration and anger where he remains calm and tender. Oh, that through the help of his Holy Spirit we would easily imitate this amazing attribute of God!

Patience displays not only our faith in, and imitation of, the One who has been so patient with us in our sinful and ugly ways, but it also displays our trust in him. When you trust God, you aren't prone to impatience, because impatience stems from not getting what you want. When you trust God, what you want is his will alone, and impatience is less and less of an issue. Impatience implies that God has lost control; that things have happened that weren't meant to happen, and that life is out of whack. But for the believer who trusts in God's complete sovereignty, there is nothing that is too late, too slow, or unwelcome, because we know that it all first passes through the hand of God (see Lam. 3:38). When you are assured of this truth, you are set free from the bondage of impatience that prompts you to become controlling, critical, doubtful, fearful, or just plain restless. The restlessness of impatience that grinds on your gut and panics your mind is the opposite of resting in the Lord, of finding strength in his peaceful patience and his sovereignty over even our little inconveniences and catastrophes.

Patience is the enemy of self, and this is as it should be. *Patience denies self, gives it no voice, subdues it and insists that it wait its turn,* something self is never good at. But the fruit of patience teaches self its proper place, the grave. God never intended for your self-life to lead your redeemed life, but to die to it. In Colossians we read to *"put to death . . . what is earthly in you"* (Col. 3:5). And all of God's commands center on this one concept, denying self that you might take up your cross daily and follow Jesus (Matt. 16:24), obey him and him alone, refusing through the power of the Spirit to give in to the demands of self on the grounds that self is attempting to steal the seat on the throne of your life. We cannot, after all, serve two masters (Matt. 6:24), not even self and God. One must die in us. But do not fear. The flame of this self-death doesn't hurt what is righteous in you, but only what is sinful, as you die to live.[7]

Just Be Patient

It has been a great benefit to me, not only as a source of my initial strength for patience in trials but also in aftermath of my failure to be patient, to consider tests of my patience to be administered by God rather than by man. When I see each test as coming directly from him, I see that he is teaching me to rest in him, to trust him, and to refuse to worship anything or anyone other than him. So then, even as my temperature rises with impatience, the Spirit can quickly subdue the undercurrent of anger and frustration by reminding me that what God desires is my patience over my deadline, my calm heart over my hurried schedule, and my genuine love over my preferred plans for those I love. **When we see God over the difficulty, we find the patience over the impatience.**

Talk Less

The first thing that I want to do when I'm impatient is to talk. I want to tell my husband why I'm feeling the way I'm feeling. If my husband talks too slowly, I want him to get to the point. If he's not taking out the garbage quickly enough, I want to ask him a second time to get on it. My impatience looks for relief in words, and lots of them. But I find most often that words, especially in abundance, get me into trouble. Oftentimes they hurt the ones who hear them or worsen an already tense situation. After all, *"A fool gives full vent to his spirit, but a wise man quietly holds it back"* (Prov. 29:11). As you begin to resist responding to your spirit in favor of responding to his, you will find that your need for words decreases because your need to be heard subsides. This is because your desire to hear his gentle and quiet voice is more important. And in this patience blooms.

Be Patient with God

For many women, trusting their husband can be a challenge, not because of their lack of faith but because of his lack of accomplishment. Time after time, he hasn't done what he should or what he said, so to remain patient in an area of repeated failure is a tall order. But impatience speaks more to our failure to trust and be patient with God than with man. When God's will is your only desire, and when you trust him to lead not only you but also your husband, this bleeds over into your marriage. Your faith in God and your trust in him is the true source of patience with the failures of your husband.

The Holy Spirit is consistent in reminding women who will listen that God has put their husband as their head, just as Christ is the head of the church (Eph. 5:23). In so doing, your patience rests on God's faithfulness rather than man's, and here patience is much more readily found.

Allow Him to Be a Mirror

The older I get, the less I like looking in the mirror, especially when the lights are bright. The closer I look and the brighter the lights, the more imperfections I see. Mirrors, while beneficial and pleasurable to some, can be uncomfortable when they reveal something unattractive. That's why marriage can be such a hotbed for arguments and anger—a husband is the closest thing to a spiritual mirror you will ever find. Since they are so close to you and know you so well, they are prone to expose some of your ugly emotions. Emotions such as bitterness, anger, resentment, and impatience all can get a workout when you live so close to someone. But the Holy Spirit helps us to use our husband as a mirror into our souls, showing us where we have the stain of anger or rebellion on our face. As this happens we begin to identify the sin in our lives, not so that we can condemn ourselves but so that we can present our sin to God and accept his gracious forgiveness and love.

The Holy Spirit prompts us to eagerly use our husband to lead us into a better understanding of our sinful nature rather than argue against his leadership (Eph. 5:24). None of us, if looking at ourselves in holy humility, would say there is no sin in us that needs to be pointed out. As we become willing to be humiliated in the identification of our sin, by our husband and by our own emotions when we argue and disagree with him, we become less impatient with him, and instead see any minor disruptions to our comfort as potentially essential to our righteousness and perfection. In essence, the Holy Spirit allows our interactions, problems, and disagreements to prove our sinfulness, which his Word confirms in Romans 3:11, rather than to prove our rightness. And the result is a supernatural patience with the man who can become one of the best tools in the Carpenter's hand.

Allow Him to Be Wrong

Our impatience often leads us to accuse, correct, or in other ways reprove our husband, but when we can be comfortable allowing him to be wrong and trusting God to speak to him, patience comes easy. When you think that God can change and teach only you, then you prove your lack of faith not only in your husband but in God. **No wife ever changed her husband as well as the wife who prayerfully left it all up to God.** When you correct or teach your husband, your voice is likely unloving and disrespectful, and then you weaken not only his leadership and manliness but also your love for him. It is because of our disdain for his error that we grow impatient. When we demand his perfection, we are destined for disappointment because he has no capacity for perfection.

Prioritize

As a Type A personality, you would expect me to keep lists, to prioritize and organize, and you would be right, but it's not all bad. Prioritizing has given me a lot of freedom from the chains that hold me and make me impatient when everything doesn't get done. And prioritizing can help you too. Before I sat down with Michael and talked about our priorities, I was forever frazzled, feeling compelled to do it all, in order to have it all and be it all. Once we sat down and compared notes, and I found out what was most important to him, the pressure was off, and life got more pleasurable. In our discussion, Michael prioritized the goings-on in my life. First and most important is my relationship with God. The time I spend with God in the mornings is the most important time of the day and not to be missed; on this we both agreed. Next comes caring for our daughter and my husband. Then comes my writing, and last but not least comes housework. This simple prioritized list—God, family, writing, housework—brought me much relief from impatience. When once I knew my husband expected that there would be days when, because of the first three things on the list, the last thing didn't get done, I was less anxious and more patient. Knowing I didn't have to rush everyone in order to get everything done was a healthy step on the path to patience.

Many women today are overly busy and therefore low on patience. Their schedules don't allow for patience; there is too much for one woman to do. If your life has you going in too many directions, let me be the first to tell you that you don't have to do everything or "have it all." Sit down with your husband and set your priorities and decide what's most important to you both, then learn to let the less important things slide. If you value God the most, then you will look for areas where you are prone to the sin of busyness and impatience and ask the Spirit to remove them so that what is most important in your life is bringing God glory. If there are things in your life that encourage or lead to sin, then you must give yourself permission to eliminate them, even if doing so disappoints others in one way or another. The life verse for this problem, which I have often administered to myself, is found in Galatians 1:10, which says, *"For am I now seeking the approval of man, or of God? Or am I trying to please man? If I were still trying to please man, I would not be a servant of Christ."* Please God by prioritizing your life!

Quit Complaining

In an effort to turn the tide from impatience to patience we must quit complaining. These words should be tattooed on the inside of my eyelids: *"Do everything without complaining or arguing"* (Phil. 2:14 GOD'S WORD). I have dismissed this instruction and allowed complaint to nourish my impatience too many times to count. If we would continually be mindful of the sinfulness of complaint, we would find not only more patience in our life but also more joy in our husbands, who find that our complaints pierce their hearts like swords. **Complaint doesn't benefit the speaker or the hearer but poisons the water for both. Complaint accuses both God and man of not providing for woman.** One of the best gifts we can give our husbands, then, is our contentment, not our complaining and moaning. Feed your patience and his soul as you seek the Spirit to disallow complaint to be an acceptable form of communication.

Abolish Your Law

And finally, in order to gain patience, you must take an honest look at the unspoken law you have within your heart with regard to those you love, especially your husband. Which ideas are game changers for you? Which things does he have to do in order for you to respect, admire, love, and serve him? When you find those things, abolish them, because they are your own law and not a part of God's law. God's law puts no conditions on love but entreats us to love everyone (Matt. 22:39), especially the unlovable (Matt. 5:46), the mean (Matt. 5:44), the selfish (Matt. 5:49), and the ugly (James 2:8–9).

When we first got married—and you're gonna laugh—my law was that I needed a massage every night in order to feel loved. So when Michael either didn't offer that or didn't give it wholeheartedly, I considered it a cardinal sin, so to speak. I resented his lack of love, as I defined it. But over time I started to see that nowhere in the Bible does God command the husband to rub the wife's back or feet on a daily basis in order to prove his love, unfortunately! I started to let go of Hayley's law and to live for God's, and as I did, our love life improved, as well as his massages! Who would have thunk it, but after breaking my law into pieces and choosing God's selfless definition of love, patience became an attainable trait in my life. I encourage you to identify the areas in your life where you have unspoken or even spoken rules for those you love, and to check them against Scripture to make sure they are there, and to dismiss any that aren't. When you do, I promise that patience will be the beautiful and bountiful outcome for all.

Cling to God

When I consider all that needs to be done in my life—this book, the homeschool work, the housework—I can get overwhelmed. How can I do all of this? You may be feeling the same about the fruit of the Spirit. How can I do all this? The task seems daunting. But the fruit is really just the outpouring of another work—the work of clinging to God. That is the primary work for fruit to be produced. As we cling to him, as we worship him, pray to him, study his Word, and spend time in his presence, his Spirit animates our lives. He fills our hearts and our minds with the things of God, and then the fruit grows big and juicy. It grows healthy and strong, and it grows on the strength of the Holy Spirit. The task at hand for the believer is to *"seek first the kingdom of God and his righteousness, and all these things will be added to you*" (Matt. 6:33). The truth is that through becoming mindful of the need of the fruit of the Spirit, by seeing where it is lacking, and by desiring more of it in our lives, we become driven to go to the source of it.

We cannot produce the healthy, life-giving fruit without him. And we cannot fully get to him unless we cling to him, remain in him, abide in him (John 15). To cling means to stay in close contact. It means to be like a child who won't stray from her mother's side, who clings to her leg and insists on always being next to her. My daughter had those moments, especially as a toddler, where she wouldn't let me go. She refused to be peeled from my side. This is the beautiful image of a child who knows she is powerless without her parent. While many parents are annoyed by a clinging child, God is not! When we are mindful of our nothingness, we know our powerlessness. When we see his awesomeness, we run as fast as we can into his arms and refuse to be peeled away, and he is pleased. We sit at his feet with an arm around his leg, watching the world around us, knowing that because he is within our grasp we are safe, and life is a beautiful thing.

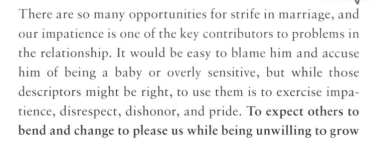

As for that in the good soil, they are those who, hearing the word, hold it fast in an honest and good heart, and bear fruit with patience. —Luke 8:15

There are so many opportunities for strife in marriage, and our impatience is one of the key contributors to problems in the relationship. It would be easy to blame him and accuse him of being a baby or overly sensitive, but while those descriptors might be right, to use them is to exercise impatience, disrespect, dishonor, and pride. **To expect others to bend and change to please us while being unwilling to grow** up spiritually ourselves is to be self-obsessed and faithless. The fruit of the Spirit is never selfish but always selfless. It is never demanding but always serving. **Patience subdues self in favor of God**, listening to the Spirit's promptings instead of our own.

But the fruit of the Spirit is
KINDNESS

 5 KINDNESS

*Kindness is me giving up my right
to hurt you for hurting me.*

—HAYLEY DIMARCO

*The meek accept injuries from men, knowing that
these are permitted by God for their ultimate good.*

—NEW BIBLE DICTIONARY

All of my life I have been a "victim" of mean girls. In high school I was tortured by most of the girls in my school. They did mean things, hurtful things, that should have broken me but just made me stronger. I was always different from other girls in many ways. I was tall for my age, skinny, with long blonde hair I wore in pigtails high on the sides of my head. I was shy and goofy. One year I vowed to wear nothing but pink, every single day of school—weird, I know. But I was smart; I got straight As. I didn't play sports like all the other girls, so I was the odd girl out. To make matters worse, the boys liked me. The girls all talked about me every day. They had a secret nickname for me, Bunny, and one night, while I was at my boyfriend's house, they came over and spray-painted mean things about "Bunny" all over his mom's drive-way! It was embarrassing and mean.

As I moved into my college years I was glad to get away from the madness but, scarred by those experiences, I chose only to make friends with guys. At least they showed me kindness. I hobbled along for many years just making things work but never having or building any lasting relationships with women.

Even as I moved into the workforce I found that women were just as catty and mean. I felt judged and written off, sensing their dislike for me, and it made me sad and even mad. I wasn't a bad person, but they all judged me as such and wrote me off. It wasn't till years later when I wrote my second book, *Mean Girls,* that I started finding some biblical answers. As I researched and wrote that book, I discovered something about myself: I was not a kind person. Sure, on the surface I was a "nice" girl. I didn't sleep around; I wasn't harsh or catty. I didn't TP houses, call people names, or try to steal girls' boyfriends. But I judged others. I was raised to distrust people, so I became an island of sorts. Encouraged to be self-confident I relied on no one and so built relationships with no one. My self-protection became, for me, a sort of unkindness because I held myself back from others, never approaching them, reaching out to them, or caring for them. Instead, I took on life as a force to be reckoned with, and while boys and men understood and related well to this kind of personality, it left little room to connect with women.

My shyness looked like standoffishness and arrogance, I'm sure. Because of my fear of women, I was distant and disconnected. In each new social encounter, I protected and hid myself. Not that my conduct is an excuse for their cruelty, but I don't have to answer for them when I stand before the Father. I only have to answer for my own conduct. Looking back now, I can see that I have never made it easy for women to feel comfortable around me. Learning to think and act like a man from early on in my life, I never developed the social skills of a female and so unconsciously alienated myself from the very people God intended for me to have some of my deepest relationships with.

What Is Kindness?

All those years, if you would have asked me if I was kind, I would undoubtedly have said yes. I felt kind, I cared about people, but I just didn't express it. I harbored no bad feelings toward others but offered no good feelings either. My kindness was always buried in my flesh, so my kind thoughts never manifested into kind actions. So allow me to offer up some more sobering conversation on the truth about kindness as a fruit not of our humanity and emotional life but as a fruit of the Spirit of God.

A powerful synonym for the kindness made possible by the Spirit of God is *grace*. Grace beautifully explains the idea of the "fruit of the Spirit" kindness. Unlike the words we might normally associate with kindness, words like *nice*, *sweet*, or even *good*, *grace* makes something deeper of kindness, something harder and more challenging to the human heart but more in keeping with the Spirit of God to whom this grace giving generally applies. Grace, as we probably all know, is the unmerited favor, divine mercy, or selfless lovingkindness shown by God to his sinful children. It was a kindness shown to us even while we were still enemies of God, dead in our own sinfulness (Eph. 2:1–5). This extreme grace, given with the aim of receiving nothing in return, is the ultimate example of kindness and the model of what it should look like in our lives.

In his Sermon on the Mount, Jesus gave us a peek at the way kindness resembles grace. As we saw in the love chapter, Jesus said, "*If you love those who love you, what reward do you have? Do not even the tax collectors do the same?*" To that, then, he adds on this very practical example of kindness when he says, "*And if you greet only your brothers, what more are you doing than others? Do not even the Gentiles do the same?*" (Matt. 5:46–47). In both of these instances Jesus is showing us that true love and kindness aren't about loving or being kind to those who are loving or kind to us in return. But our kindness to others is based on something far greater, his kindness or grace to us.

So then, **kindness is merciful**, which means it doesn't give people what they really deserve—distrust, retaliation, or rejection—but what they don't deserve—compassion, sympathy, and forgiveness. Kindness isn't generated from the goodness or beauty of the person we offer it to but from the Spirit of God, who is the very gift of grace to those who believe.

It is easy to be kind to people who don't offend us and who agree with us, love us, and never cross us, but when we are kind to the unlovely, the mean, and the difficult, we are responding to the grace of God within us, allowing it to flow from us to them. This fruit of kindness is tenderhearted. It is slow to anger, and the one who offers it considers her own sinfulness and failure as evidence that there is no one righteous and therefore no one who isn't going to mess up. There is no doubt, as we look at the grace of God, that it is generous, and the same is meant to be true for the grace God wants us to share with others. *Gracious* is a beautiful description of the person whose life is filled with the fruit of kindness. Rather than expecting something in return for kindness, as "I will be kind to you if you will be kind to me," grace offers itself expecting nothing in return, giving to those who don't even deserve it.

Kindness Killers

While you may feel like the kindest person in the world, kindness has more to do with how the people around you feel about you than how you feel about them. If I am honest about the relationships I've built, what people from my past would say about me, I think most would not remember my kindness. My inability to put myself in the shoes of others, to consider them when I speak, dress, and do the things I do, is breathtaking, and not in a good way. From dressing without considering the spiritual lives of the men around me, to criticizing people "for their own good," I've been all kinds of unkind. So, as I make this list, I don't include any of these things with a finger pointing at my readers but rather at myself. Thank God for his grace and the amazing power of confession to heal the confessor! All I can say is that I hope that my failure at kindness will somehow speak to you and help you to move more in the direction of our perfect Savior, whose kindness was beyond compare.

Our Sense of Justice

The way I see it, there are two major categories of kindness killers: our sense of justice and our fear of rejection, both of which pour out of our failure to abide. Kindness has little to do with merit but much to do with grace. It also has little to do with reward but much to do with favor. Like the other fruit of the Spirit, kindness is meant to nourish those around us, regardless of how well they nourish us in return. Unfortunately, many of us struggle with a strong sense of justice with regard to how we are being treated. We look at evil or even difficulty in our lives and our sense of pride screams for judgment, retribution, and discipline on the unfairness going on. Knowing, as we do so well, good from evil, when we sense anything but good, we immediately begin to move toward our flesh and the application of our own force, attempting to balance the situation. In this desire for justice, we step in and get to work toward what we sense is needed.

In all of this then, we are prone first of all to unkindness, to judging others' need for punishment and/or correction. In other words, when someone does something wrong, says something mean, or in anyway acts unkindly, we determine that the most just response from us is the same thing. This is the way we behave when we say, "But he started it."

When our husband is unkind, when he refuses to love us the way he should according to Ephesians 5:28, which we know by heart, we begin to make excuses for our own lack of fruit. We may be quick to anger and start right in arguing our case for his injustice, fighting to prove ourselves right. We may choose to shut up and give him the silent treatment for a few days, teaching him a lesson, which unwittingly is, "My grace (read: kindness), unlike God's, is completely dependent on your goodness." We may hold a grudge and refuse to get over something he has done. We might just withhold something that we know he loves, like sex, in order to teach him never to do that thing again. We may be unsympathetic in our disdain for his unbelievably sinful nature, which is so unlike our own and so deserving of our ridicule and sarcasm. Or what he did might be so horrible that it can never be forgiven, and so we withhold from him the very core of the grace that God has given us, forgiveness, on the grounds that his sin was too big to forgive.

What ultimately our sense of justice is fighting for isn't holiness but self-protection. In all of these "offenses" against us, it is what they do to our own emotional life that compels us to seek retribution. When we are hurt by an offense, our natural response is fight or flight. In the fight, we remain and attempt to bring him to his knees so that he can see the error of his ways and love us properly. In flight, we run off and hide, hoping that this maneuver will lead him to some sense of remorse, understanding, and contrition. And in both scenarios we are hoping to protect ourselves.

The Fear of Rejection

Beyond a sense of justice and offense is a level of fear. The fear of rejection can lead us to miss opportunities to show kindness.

Kindness requires moving out of yourself, a risk taking if you will. There are plenty of risks in being kind; we might be rejected, laughed at, or made fun of, which can keep a lot of us, especially shy types, from reaching out and acting in the same kind of daring grace that Christ demonstrated when he came to earth.

Unfortunately, many of us have been hurt by this world, wounded by the words and actions of others, and because of that we have hardened our hearts in order to protect ourselves from future pain of rejection. For many years I worked at this process like a skilled laborer, building a clever wall around my heart so that no one could ever again hurt me the way my father did when he abandoned me at the tender age of twelve. I determined always to protect myself. I shut myself off from any risk to my heart, and in so doing I damaged myself more than my father ever could.

A hard heart is the opposite of a tender heart. This hardness is meant to keep ourselves from getting used, damaged, or destroyed ever again. But in the pursuit of self-protection, self becomes our object of affection, our idol that must be protected and cherished above all else. **In this broken state, God takes a backseat to our wounds and our precious heart.** We see kindness, then, as an enemy rather than as gracious disregard for worthiness. But **the grace of God that is the fruit of his Spirit in us isn't the grace of reserve or self-protection but of surrender and self-abandonment.** It was Christ, after all, who gave up everything in order to give grace to each one of us. It was he who risked the pain of torture and death, of love and it's most certain rejection in order to show us his kindness. If he would risk a broken heart, why would we not joyfully risk the same? His wounds, after all, are far more significant than ours, and far more important, as they were meant to heal all our past, present, and future wounds.

Before you allow your woundedness and fear of rejection to trump the grace you give others, remember that God created the world knowing that the price for that creation would ultimately be the torture and death of his Son. He gave life to mankind, knowing full well the magnitude of rejection that we would wield against him time and again. Yet he did not allow that truth to destroy his kindness and to erase the existence of mankind from the cosmos. Instead, he marched forward, graciously accepting our rejection as part and parcel of his love for us. To not do the same for those he's put in our lives is to hold our own hearts in higher regard than his. When we fear rejection and clutch so tightly to our wounds, that is exactly what we do.

Kindness must bear with the sins of others, give generously, and show mercy. When we are without mercy, we are without kindness and grace. Mercy requires us to be fearless when it comes to giving ourselves, because showing mercy allows people to hurt us again. It can feel like mercy is giving people permission to continue to hurt you. Yet mercy isn't meant to destroy but to bring life. Our mercy reveals God's mercy to those with whom we freely share it. No one is more surprised by mercy than a man who knows how badly he has messed up. Mercy is rooted in kindness, because mercy, like grace, is given not on the merit of the one who messed up but on the unearned favor of the God who forgives.

Failing to Abide

Ultimately our failure in the fruit of kindness, as in everything, stems from our failure to abide in Christ. And it is through being mindful of the things of the Spirit, of who God is, what he's said and done, that we may abide. Consider these verses:

So faith comes from hearing, and hearing through the word of Christ. (Rom. 10:17)

As obedient children, do not be conformed to the passions of your former ignorance. (1 Pet. 1:14)

My people are destroyed for lack of knowledge; because you have rejected knowledge, I reject you from being a priest to me. And since you have forgotten the law of your God, I also will forget your children. (Hos. 4:6)

Too often in the life of faith, we believe that abiding in Christ and living in the Spirit should come easily, naturally. But abiding in Christ is not possible without hearing his supernatural voice, which is the Word of God.

And so, for many, **it's neither justice nor fear that keeps us from kindness, but simple ignorance of what God has said and done.** And that's why an ignorance of who God is prevents us from abiding and living a life that bears spiritual fruit, which includes biblical kindness. And it's from this ignorance that we start defining words like *kindness* through our flesh. For instance, as long as your definition of kindness involves what you get out of it, like love or acceptance, it's fruit-of-the-flesh kindness and not the grace kind of stuff we are talking about. Until we know that kindness isn't just about being friendly to those who are friendly to us but about showing kindness when hate or indifference is given in return, when anger erupts or when we're simply unappreciated, we can't fully grow in the fruit of kindness.

I can claim this one. I had no idea what kindness entailed. I knew nothing of grace and so I knew nothing of fearless love or compassionate mercy. When we are untrained in the ways of faith—the words of Deuteronomy 6:7–9, "*You shall teach them diligently to your children, and shall talk of them when you sit in your house, and when you walk by the way, and when you lie down, and when you rise. You shall bind them as a sign on your hand, and they shall be as frontlets between your eyes. You shall write them on the doorposts of your house and on your gates"*—then we continue in ignorance of the abounding goodness of the fruit that the Spirit wants to produce in our lives, and kindness easily becomes something that it isn't. And we become, without even realizing it, unkind women.

Many of us have trained ourselves in the area of frugality, working hard to be measured in our use of stuff. And while this is admirable and beneficial to the home, it can also be easily perverted into unkindness. **When we are devoted to frugality we can often make the principle of lack more important than the grace and beauty of abundance.** In other words, when we put so much emphasis on saving money, on protecting and caring for our stuff, we convey a notion of lack and a need to guard what little we have. But our God is a God of abundance, and in this abundance we should generously give what little we have, knowing full well that God will provide for the loss. We give our husbands the food they ask for, even if it seems to us to be too decadent. We allow our kids to be kids and to play freely in the home rather than scream and shout about the importance of our stain-free carpet. And we offer ourselves and our time because we aren't our own but our Father's. And in this we move from stingy to generous and from unkindness to kindness.

Remember the fact that he is the owner of the cattle on a thousand hills (Ps. 50:10). Nothing is out of his reach, nothing doesn't belong to him. And that includes everything we own. When the Holy Spirit animates your life, he brings you away from your stingy attachment to stuff and moves you out in the openhandedness of grace. In your ignorance, perhaps you have put too much emphasis on guarding your stuff and protecting your things and have called it "stewardship," but knowing what you know now, may you freely open your fingers and allow your stuff to be used by God for his glory, whether that means its removal from your life or even its destruction. Another thing we sometimes fail to consider is the importance of gratitude. **Kindness is grateful, quickly saying thank you, knowing that giving thanks is both a humble and a generous way of feeding the hearts of those around us, especially our men.** But many of us are ignorant of the importance of the two words *thank you* to the men in our lives. The two simple words *thank you* mean so much to their masculine hearts. It is a good way to appreciate them for all that they do and bring to your life, and an easy and quick act of kindness goes a long way.

God's Kind Commandments

The truth is that **all our kindness is predicated by God's kindness to us.** He is to be our example, which we read in Luke 6:35: *"But love your enemies, and do good, and lend, expecting nothing in return, and your reward will be great, and you will be sons of the Most High, for he is kind to the ungrateful and the evil."* It is the ultimate form of arrogance to accept all of God's graciousness, all of his lovingkindness, forgiveness, and irrevocable grace and then to be unkind, ungracious, and harsh with others, even if they are ungrateful and evil. I cannot say it any better than this: *"You have no excuse, O man, every one of you who judges. For in passing judgment on another you condemn yourself, because you, the judge, practice the very same things. . . . Do you presume on the riches of his kindness and forbearance and patience, not knowing that God's kindness is meant to lead you to repentance?"* (Rom. 1:2–4).

It is important for us all to remember that being kind to our enemies—those who oppose us or seek to harm us in some way—is hard, especially if your "enemy" is your husband. But we all once were enemies to God, and yet while we were his enemies, he showed us grace and reconciled us to himself (Rom. 5:10). He didn't hold our enemy status against us but graciously forgave us all our sins, showing compassion, mercy, and love. This is why, then, as his children, we are commanded to put on *"as God's chosen ones, holy and beloved, compassionate hearts, kindness, humility, meekness, and patience, bearing with one another and, if one has a complaint against another, forgiving each other; as the Lord has forgiven you, so you also must forgive. And above all these put on love, which binds everything together in perfect harmony"* (Col. 3:12–14).

The idea of forgiveness is probably the hardest part of kindness, but it is vital. **If you consider the synonym of *kindness* to be *grace*, then you can't help but remember that forgiveness walks hand in hand with it,** and that *"if you do not forgive others their trespasses, neither will your Father forgive your trespasses"* (Matt. 6:15). This is a crucial connection. Grace and forgiveness are inseparable. But how easy it is to claim an incapacity to forgive what we can't forget. After all, it would be hypocrisy, wouldn't it, to say, "You are forgiven," but still have the memory of it in your mind? Because of this and our strong sense of justice, many of us refuse to forgive and so refuse to live in the graciousness of Holy Spirit kindness. But those words in Matthew 6:15 should be our inspiration. Erased memories aren't essential for forgiveness, but your forgiveness is an essential mark that you have received his forgiveness (see Matt. 18:23–35). And it is an integral part of practicing kindness.

The instructions for kindness in the life of faith are not just for our own testing but for far greater purposes, both of which have to do not with us but with God. **The first and most important reason that kindness is meant to be a part of the life of faith is that it is a part of the Father's character** and serves a great purpose in the lives of his children. **His kindness is meant to lead us to repentance** (Rom. 2:4). **And our kindness is meant to lead others to him.** What kind of a witness is it when his children are unkind, unmerciful, and judgmental? What do our actions and words say about him? The fruitful wife considers this and also knows that her kindness serves many purposes, one of which is that it reveals the love of God to her husband, and so encourages him and builds him up in his faith. Kindness is a generous gift. Ultimately, *"whatever you do, in word or deed, do everything in the name of the Lord Jesus, giving thanks to God the Father through him"* (Col. 3:17). When we act in kindness toward our husband, we do it in the name of the Lord Jesus, and we bring him glory.

Becoming a Grace Giver

It's sometimes easier to show kindness to complete strangers or acquaintances than to those who are closest to us. How much easier it is to be short, distant, or unforgiving with your husband than with the clerk at the checkout line? Sure, there are moments when a short fuse causes you to roll your eyes at a person who cuts in line in front of you, but the most persistent rejection of God's call to show grace occurs in our treatment of those we are most intimate with.

My mother and I are very close; in fact, she lives with us, so we see each other every day. I can honestly say that it is oftentimes harder to offer grace to her than to one hundred people I meet on the street. With her I am prone to be short-tempered, harsh, and intolerant. And I can be the same way toward my husband. Since most of us have a hard time being "on" all the time, we let loose at home, and our family gets to experience it all.

When it comes to kindness, most of us probably think it has to do with being nice, hospitable, and friendly, and while those things are indeed an afterglow from a faithful life, the fruit of kindness goes deeper.

Allow Him to Make Mistakes

As women saved by grace from too many sins to count, when we recall what Jesus has done for us it becomes natural to graciously allow our husband to make his own mistakes. In those moments of testing, God's grace toward us helps us keep from rolling our eyes when he's wrong, making fun of him, complaining about him, or reminding him of his failures. Through the power of the Holy Spirit we can still love him even though he is imperfect, just like the Father loves us. **It is a work of the Spirit to love a man not because of what he does or doesn't do.** After all, we recall, it is *"by grace you have been saved through faith. And this is not your own doing; it is the gift of God, not a result of works, so that no one may boast"* (Eph. 2:8–9). The mind set on the things of the Spirit knows that if your husband has to work hard for your grace when God's is freely given, then something is terribly wrong. There are no works that can earn God's love, and there should be no works your husband must do to earn yours. **As thanks for God's mercy, compassion, and grace we all must offer grace to our husbands as they fail to be the men we want them to be.**

Get Over It

In marriage there are moments of great testing, pain, and struggle—moments when he hurts us, when he fails us, and when he sins against us—but consider that without these moments, kindness wouldn't be dependent on the Spirit; it could manage quite well in the power of the flesh. These moments of testing are the proving ground for the fruit of the Spirit, because these moments are what prove that the fruit is unnatural to the branch but fully reliant on the vine. In these times, the Holy Spirit compels us to quickly get over our husband's mistakes. **Because kindness can't exist in the midst of**

resentment or grudge, the Spirit gives us the skill of getting over things. To get over something is to refuse to act on memories that lead us to sin. To get over something is to choose kindness over getting even. In our fight for justice, it can be easy to want equality so badly that we try to balance out his sin by giving him some of our own. But when we are keenly aware of God's thoughts on kindness through the counsel of the Holy Spirit and his Word, then we can let go of our sense of justice and trust God with everything, even our own pain.

Do not say, "I will repay evil"; wait for the Lord, and he will deliver you. —Proverbs 20:22

Don't Keep a Record of Wrongs

One of the most amazing things about God's kindness is that he doesn't keep a tally of our mistakes. He removes them as far as the east is from the west, and his Spirit helps us to offer the same kindness as we refuse to keep a record of our husband's wrongs. It's so easy to keep a mental note of all the times your husband has failed you and then use that to decide how you're going to treat him. I find myself subconsciously doing the same thing: "Well, he didn't do what I wanted so I'm not going to do what he wants." But that is me responding to the promptings of the flesh, not the Spirit. When a woman has her mind set on the things of the Spirit, she finds no need to use her husband's mistakes against him, or the relationship, but in humility she is able to let go and move on in holy kindness.

Don't Punish Him as His Sins Deserve

When you consider kindness, you must take note of the fact that God's kindness removed the punishment that our sins deserved. This kind of kindness can be uncomfortable for the woman who has to give it, because it removes any opportunity to correct through punishment. As natural as it is for parents to punish their child for wrongdoing, so it can be for a woman to punish her husband—yet kindness isn't about punishment but about mercy. When he sins, we feel justified in our desire to punish him, but **if God, who is rich in mercy** (Eph. 2:4), **doesn't punish him as his sins deserve, then what makes our justice more strenuous than his?**

Forgive Him Over and Over

One of the hardest things to do is to forgive someone who steps on your toes 490 times, but that is exactly what God wants from us when he says that we are to forgive others seventy times seven, meaning without limit (Matt. 18:21–22). It is human nature to not to want to be taken for a fool, and so we tend to demand growth and change in others before offering forgiveness. But even if there is no change, and he continues to mess up in the same way, the kindness of the Spirit prompts us to forgive him as the Father has forgiven us. How many times, certainly more than seven times seventy, has God forgiven me for my prayerlessness, pride, and selfishness? So when I can't forgive Michael for failing to do what I asked him to do, I'm rejecting the grace the Holy Spirit wants me to offer.

Offering forgiveness seems like a dangerous thing to a heart that doesn't personally know the depths of God's grace. But the person who has been forgiven much finds forgiveness supernaturally easier to give. When you look at a person who needs your forgiveness through the filter and power of the Holy Spirit, kindness takes hold of your heart.

Give Him More Than He Deserves

A big part of kindness is moving away from the concept of equity or fairness. The life of kindness was never meant to be fair; if it was, then God couldn't offer any of us grace, because we have nothing to offer in return. But kindness is a big giver, giving much more than is deserved, and the same is true in marriage. There are times and seasons when we women give much more than our husbands give. When these times come, when we can see that we work harder and give more, it can be easy to focus on the unfairness of it all. We can question if we aren't doing more in the marriage than he deserves us to do, but kindness isn't predicated on the action but on the inaction of others. The fruit of the Spirit kind of kindness shows up in those moments when he doesn't deserve it, when we are doing much more. **Kindness doesn't always pay off for the giver, but it wasn't meant to.** Kindness isn't about the giver but about the receiver, and it isn't about us but about the Father, whose character we seek to imitate in order that he may be glorified.

Apologize Quickly

An apology is a beautiful thing, especially when it's offered to me! But if you ask me to apologize, I'm just sorry that you're such a sensitive person. And I'm sorry you think I did something wrong. My apology is all about you, not about me, because, frankly, I didn't do anything wrong.

"I couldn't help it."

"The road was slick."

"The deadline was too quick."

"The oven was too hot."

Most of my life, I've struggled to accept blame for my sins and failures. I've blamed the circumstances instead. After all, if they had been different, then I wouldn't have failed. But tell you I was wrong or that I shouldn't have done what I did? Confess my stupidity or miscalculation to you? Are you crazy?! I can't bear such humiliation. But kindness requires quick apology. Apology that says, "It's my fault. I'm sorry. Please forgive me." These simple words are so hard for me to say. Failing to apologize is to refuse to accept responsibility for your own actions or words. It's to tell the one you wronged that his feelings don't matter. It puts pride in the center ring and shuts humility out of the room. It refuses the death that leads to sanctification and prefers fighting for its life (Rom. 6:2–7).

As we respond to the Spirit's promptings rather than to our flesh's, we apologize quickly because there is nothing in us that needs to be protected or sheltered from the embarrassment of being wrong.

* * *

When we are mindful of the Holy Spirit within us more than anything else, when we focus on who he is, what he wants, and how he loves, then giving kindness to the unlovely is easy, not because of who we are but because of who he is. We may try with all our strength to be kind but find that we keep failing. We may want to offer grace even though we continue to judge and condemn, but we can't lose heart or give up. We have to get back to the source, to run to the Father, to devote our living and breathing to him. **When we make our kindness about him and not about us, then we will find it comes so much more easily.** Kindness is the emulation of God's grace and the effect of his Spirit in our lives.

Any human heart, under its own power, can be nice and kind, but only through the fruit of the Spirit are we able to offer grace. That's the difference between human kindness and "fruit of the Spirit" kindness. *"Be kind to one another, tenderhearted, forgiving one another, as God in Christ forgave you"* (Eph. 4:32). It isn't the kindness we experience in response to the way others make us feel but the kindness we give in spite of the way others make us feel, that truly exhibits the fruit of the Spirit. When this kind of supernatural kindness is present in us, the world takes notice and sees something that makes no human sense. It sees what can happen when a woman is compelled to act according to the life of the Holy Spirit that is within her.

Corrie ten Boom exemplified supernatural kindness after her "accidental" release from the concentration camp that took the life of her sister Betsie. In 1947 she was speaking at a church in Germany on the subject of God's forgiveness. After her talk, a man whom she recognized immediately as the cruelest guard at Ravensbruck approached her with an outstretched hand. Her blood froze. She wanted to run, to get away from his gaze, from his touch. As she looked at him, she recalled the emaciated body of her sister and the whip on his belt. She knew exactly who he was, but he did not know her. He thanked her for her words on forgiveness and then proceeded to tell her that he had once been a guard at Ravensbruck and had since become a Christian. He said that he had the forgiveness of God for his cruelty to the women in the camp but would love to hear it from her as well.

Corrie was sickened by the idea that she would have to give him forgiveness, but she knew that she must, since God's Word commands it. She fumbled in her purse, trying not to meet his outstretched hand. "Will you forgive me?" he asked. In her memoir, *Tramp for the Lord*, Corrie beautifully explains what happened next:

> And so woodenly, mechanically, I thrust my hand into the one stretched out to me. And as I did, an incredible thing took place. The current started in my shoulder, raced down my arm, sprang into our joined hands. And then this healing warmth seemed to flood my whole being, bringing tears to my eyes. "I forgive you, brother!" I cried. "With all my heart." For a long moment we grasped each other's hands, the former guard and the former prisoner. I had never known God's love so intensely as I did then. But even so, I realized it was not my love. I had tried, and did not have the power. It was the power of the Holy Spirit as recorded in Romans 5:5: "God's love has been poured into our hearts through the Holy Spirit who has been given to us."[8]

Like Corrie ten Boom, it's our mindfulness of God's Word that makes us awkwardly thrust out our hand, but it's the power of his Spirit that has been poured into our hearts and pulses out in those moments of kindness and forgiveness that truly transforms lives. You too can share the grace of God with those who have hurt you, but only through the power of the Holy Spirit that fills your heart with a supernatural love.

But the fruit of the Spirit is
GOODNESS

6 GOODNESS

*Believers are placed in the world with this one
object, that they may let their light shine in
good works, so as to win men to God.*

—ANDREW MURRAY

*Let us, then, be ever mindful of our depen-
dence upon the Spirit of God. We derived our
new life from him, and only he can maintain it
in us. Without him we can neither think good
thoughts, speak good words, nor do good deeds.*

—GEORGE WASHINGTON BETHUNE

When something is good, it pleases you. Me, I'm pleased by
fresh peaches, chocolate ice cream, and a soft breeze. These
things are good in my estimation because they please me. But
everyone's definition of *good* is different. My husband thinks
bratwursts are good, and I couldn't disagree more. *Good*
and *goodness* are relative terms in this world. So what was
God talking about when he said that the fruit of the Spirit is
goodness?

Since goodness is listed as a fruit of the Spirit, we must
get our definition of it from God. Goodness is defined by God
and no one else. God defines goodness, because God is good
(1 Chron. 16:34). In fact, he's the only one who is inherently
good. Even Jesus mind-twistingly said, *"Why do you call me
good? No one is good except God alone"* (Mark 10:18). In
Psalm 115:3 we read that *"our God is in the heavens; he does
all that he pleases."* So if God is good, and everything he does
is good, and he does what he pleases, then we can conclude

that what pleases God is goodness, which we see confirmed in Psalm 11:7: "*For the* LORD *is righteous; he loves righteous deeds.*" Knowing that God is good, we can infer that goodness is what pleases God; therefore, **goodness can be defined as anything that is pleasing to God.** And where do we learn what is pleasing to God? In his Word.

Goodness Displays Our Love

This idea that loving God involves pleasing him is seen in 1 John 5:3: "*For this is the love of God, that we keep his commandments. And his commandments are not burdensome.*" D. A. Carson, in his *New Bible Commentary*, says, "Real love is shown by a concern to do God's will. Indeed John can say that *love for God* is *to obey his commands.* John is not a legalist, but he recognizes that love is busy; it finds its natural expression in doing the things that please the beloved, and where will we find these things better than in *his commands?*"[9] So goodness is seen in our conduct, thoughts, and actions. It isn't your obedience that makes you good, but his goodness and love that make you obedient, and it's this goodness that reveals our faith in him.

According to Ezekiel 36:27, it is God's Spirit that causes us to walk in his statutes and to carefully obey his rules. Unbelievers do good, whether it be through sheer determination or just plain nature, but "*without faith it is impossible to please him*" (Heb. 11:6). Therefore, they cannot grow in true goodness. Goodness comes through faith, because only in faith do we have the desire to find out what pleases God and to do it.

Certainly there are believers who fail to do good; we all, at one time or another, choose wrong over right, sin over obedience. So does that make us unfit for goodness? By no means; it only makes us rely more on the Spirit, who enables us to exhibit his goodness.

Goodness Is Imitating God

Our goodness is evidence that we belong to God. Goodness is foundational to our faith, because it imitates our Father. In Ephesians 5:1 we are called to *"be imitators of God, as beloved children."* Children who love their father want to be just like him. They are proud of him, impressed by him, and deeply want to *be* like him so that others can see the resemblance and so that their father will be proud of them and say, "Well done, my good and faithful child!" Imitation is the highest form of flattery, and it is the best evidence of relationship. The apostle Paul pointed out his imitation of God when he said to the Corinthians, *"Be imitators of me, as I am of Christ"* (1 Cor. 11:1). And God himself says to all of us, *"Be holy, for I am holy"* (Lev. 11:44).

The desire for perfection is written into the fiber of our beings. We long for perfection in the world around us, in the people we love, and within ourselves. And when we fail to find that perfection we were made for, we often resort to sinful tactics to attempt to change our imperfect condition to something more palatable. But perfection is attainable in only one place, in the life lived in Christ. This is the perfect place for us. As I think of Christ as our perfection, I am moved by these words of Oswald Chambers: "The Spirit of Jesus is conscious of one thing only—a perfect oneness with the Father, and He says 'Learn of Me, for I am meek and lowly in heart.' All I do ought to be founded on a perfect oneness with Him, not on a self-willed determination to be godly. This will mean that I can be easily put upon, easily over-reached, easily ignored; but if I submit to it for His sake, I prevent Jesus Christ being persecuted."[10]

Goodness Is Living in the Light

Goodness becomes a part of our being when oneness with the Father is the only thing we are conscious of. Because he is good, and we want only what he wants, we then find ourselves with the "fruit of the Spirit" goodness. So, goodness is imitating God, but imitating God requires an understanding of who God is.

In 1 John 1:5 we read that *"God is light, and in him is no darkness at all."* This concept of light is foundational to our understanding of goodness. Light surrounds all that is good and darkness all that is evil; therefore, God wants us to live in the light as he is in the light (1 John 1:7). As we read in Ephesians 5:8–9, *"For at one time you were darkness, but now you are light in the Lord. Walk as children of light (for the fruit of light is found in all that is good and right and true)."*

But what does it mean to live in the light? To answer that we first must remember that Jesus is light. He says this of himself in John 8:12: *"I am the light of the world. Whoever follows me will not walk in darkness, but will have the light of life."* When you follow Christ, you walk where he walks. You behave as he behaves and want what he wants. This concept of light reveals to us the nature of goodness, and goodness is manifest as we walk in the light.

The Holy Spirit, then, compels us to live in light rather than in darkness and so produces in us goodness. An essential part of living in the light is allowing the light to illuminate those areas in our lives where we have let sin creep in. This sin, hidden and living freely in darkness, is then chased off like skittish cockroaches in a dark room that is suddenly illuminated by a flip of the switch. And the way this happens spiritually is by way of confession.

Confession, the agreeing with God that we have sinned, is living in the light, as we see in Ephesians 5:11–14: *"Take no part in the unfruitful works of darkness, but instead expose them. For it is shameful even to speak of the things that they do in secret. But when anything is exposed by the light, it becomes visible, for anything that becomes visible is light. Therefore it says, 'Awake, O sleeper, and arise from the dead, and Christ will shine on you.'"* The light of Christ illuminates our sin and allows us to freely confess that we have dishonored and disobeyed God. Goodness has all the lights on and isn't afraid to show the mess to the world, because all of the mess has been covered by the blood of Christ and is forgiven.

Many of us live in the light most of the time. We have the lights on—the front porch and even the entryway and main living area are bright and lit—but there is, in the back of the house of our life, a dark room where no one enters but us, and in that room we hide our secret sins, those delicious sins that we allow ourselves now and again. But the goodness of the Holy Spirit illuminates this darkness. He shines the light on it and chases away the sin that lingers there. Goodness compels us to turn the lights on in every room and to keep nothing hidden from sight. When that is the case, even our sin is washed clean by the brightness of the light, and we are set free from the deeds of darkness. **Those who live in darkness, hiding their sin or claiming not to sin, are not practicing goodness, because they are living part of their lives in darkness, and goodness requires light.**

Confession is important. In fact, we learn that *"if we say we have not sinned, we make him a liar, and his word is not in us"* (1 John 1:10). To lie, to say that we have no sin, to hide our sin from others, or even to take pride in it as if it weren't an offense against God, is to show that the Holy Spirit doesn't animate our lives. For the Holy Spirit to do his work and to produce the fruit of goodness, we must bring all our life out into the light and look at it through the light of God's Word so that we can confess our failings and embrace his beautiful grace (1 John 1:9).

Goodness Is Living in Community

In Genesis, God created the world, and after each day of creation, he "saw that is was good." But after God created man, he saw something different. In Genesis 2:18 God saw that it was not good for the man to be alone, so God created woman. This need for community is an essential part of our humanity because it is an essential part of God's nature. God lives in community—God the Father, God the Son, and God the Holy Spirit. So community should be important to God's children, and community requires goodness, the goodness of mercy, compassion, encouragement, and edification. Goodness is good for community.

Goodness Is Satisfying

After a good meal or a good conversation, you feel satisfied. Good things bring satisfaction, or pleasure, to those who experience them, and so the fruit of goodness will be satisfying to others.

But there are a lot of things that can be dangerous to the fruit of goodness, like crankiness, quarreling, jealousy, conceit, cattiness, and even self-hatred. These things do not satisfy but frustrate. Of course, they are just emotions, and emotions are hard to manage, but goodness insists on morality rather than immorality, and anything that has as its root our sinfulness is by definition immoral.

PEOPLE PLEASERS. People pleasers believe that showing goodness to others is a requirement. Without it they fear rejection, disappointment, even anger. But people pleasers are ultimately seeking their own good, not God's. Goodness isn't meant to bring justification, acceptance, or love from man but to reflect God's love to the world. If you are a people pleaser, consider the fact that goodness must sometimes disappoint others, when it makes pleasing God more important than man (see Gal. 1:10).

So, then, the opposite of goodness is immorality, or turning away from God. While immorality makes grandiose promises for satisfaction, ultimately it fails. Goodness in marriage is a woman's commitment to seek, no matter how she may feel, to live out God's Word in her daily life, abiding in Christ, and bringing satisfaction to her husband. It's so easy in intimate relationships to get angry when others are unhappy with us, when they complain, and when they point out problems, but the fruit of goodness, in devotion to the Father, is willing to make our own satisfaction subordinate to God's will for relationships.

This goodness, the turning over of one's heart to God, satisfies not only those whom it loves, but also God himself. Your goodness gives God glory, according to Matthew 5:14–16, which speaks again about the importance of light and the believer. In this section of Scripture Jesus says, "*You are the light of the world. A city set on a hill cannot be hidden. Nor do people light a lamp and put it under a basket, but on a stand, and it gives light to all in the house. In the same way, let your light shine before others, so that they may see your good works and give glory to your Father who is in heaven.*" Your goodness, then, is a light that shines before others, pointing them to the Father.

Goodness serves as a witness not only to man but also to God, for we read in Ephesians 6:8 that the good "*anyone does, this he will receive back from the Lord.*" So, while goodness often satisfies others at our expense, we can fully expect to receive it all back from the Lord. This means that acting in goodness will ultimately be our satisfaction.

Goodness vs. the Flesh

Goodness does not come natural to us. In fact, it is completely foreign to the flesh. We know this because of Romans 8:8, which says, "*Those who are in the flesh cannot please God.*"

When we serve our flesh rather than Christ, we are driven by our feelings. We are so used to living by emotion that we oftentimes are closer to our feelings than we are to God. Goodness takes a backseat to our emotional state.

I have always had wide hormonal shifts, and once a month my mind is blown by this evil-natured chemistry that urges me to anything but goodness. What at other times is relatively easy to overcome dominates me as I lash out at anyone and everyone in my path. As I was thinking about this in the process of studying goodness, I started to ask myself what I thought. Did God only command goodness twenty days a month, as I had become accustomed? Is goodness conditional upon leveled hormones, good feelings, and happy moods? Or are the children of God called to a higher plane? A stiffer challenge? A mightier calling? I laughed as I thought about it: "Be imitators of God for twenty days a month, then for the remaining eight to ten 'bad' days, you are free to imitate Satan." Abiding in Christ is not twenty days on, eight days off! Why had I given myself a free pass? "It's just that time of the month. Everybody stay out of my way!" What a silly girl I am.

Goodness vs. Evil Treasures

Our failure to exhibit the fruit of goodness comes in large part because of where our hearts are and what they covet. When we covet the things of this world, when we covet ease of life, comfort, or happiness, we no longer treasure the things of God, and where our heart is, there our fruit lies. As we read in Matthew 12:35, "*The good person out of his good treasure brings forth good, and the evil person out of his evil treasure brings forth evil.*" The question we all have to ask is, what do I treasure? If we don't have a whole lot of the fruit of goodness in our lives, then our treasures might be the problem. But a heart turned over to God, finding its treasure in him alone, is a heart overflowing with goodness. In this way the

Holy Spirit does his work in you and produces an abundance of good fruit.

Goodness vs. Fear

Unfortunately, many of us don't see God moving fast enough, so we panic and start to take matters into our own hands. When we do this, the fruit of goodness is stifled by the flesh that fights alongside it. Goodness is oftentimes uncomfortable for us, because goodness involves surrendering ourselves to the life of Christ in us. Goodness imitates Christ—Christ who didn't think that equality with God was a thing to be grasped at, but emptied himself by taking on the form of a servant, being born a man (Phil. 2:6–7). I often marvel at the apparent ease with which Christ lived life. It all seemed so effortless, the walking, the talking, the healing, even the slipping off to be alone with the Father. But Christ was 100 percent man, as well as 100 percent God, and that means that he experienced the same pain and suffering that man experiences, perhaps even more (Heb. 4:15). Yet Christ never let fear overcome or lead him, and if we are united to him by faith, so it can be with us. But when we let fear become bigger in our minds and hearts than God, "the fruit of the Spirit" goodness is frustrated.

I have experienced the power of fear firsthand and been tortured by it. Most of my life I have let the fear of disaster control me, especially natural disaster. I have been terrified of things like earthquakes and tornadoes. I have doubted the ability of planes to get me where I want to go without crashing. And I have stressed about fires in my house while I was out. But once I realized that my safety is always in God's hands and that I can trust God's goodness no matter what, I was set free from the death grip of fear and opened up to the beauty of the "fruit of the Spirit" goodness.

Goodness vs. Darkness

I've already covered the topic of light, but I want to add that for some of us the darkness is more comfortable than the light. When that is the case, goodness is hard to come by, because goodness and darkness are incompatible. If you are unwilling to walk in the light in any area of your life, then you are unwilling to live by the Spirit, and the result is a minor, if not major, disaster. For this, we must prayerfully examine our lives in order to be mindful of the Spirit's uncovering lingering darkness and then begin to confess that darkness to a righteous friend so that we may be healed (James 5:16).

Growing in Goodness

Like all other fruit of the Spirit, goodness comes from the Holy Spirit himself, yet many of us have evidenced little of the fruit in our lives. This is not because the Spirit is lacking but because we are slow to grow in the Spirit. We all are at different stages of growth, and therefore all manifest differing degrees of fruit. When I first came face-to-face with my disturbing lack of fruit, I immediately questioned my salvation. How could I have the Spirit with little or no fruit? Isn't the fruit evidence of the life of the Spirit within me? But after I calmed down and began to search God's Word, I began to see the truth that my lack of fruit didn't mean I didn't have the Spirit of God in my life. I realized I hadn't, until then, believed that the nine fruit of the Spirit were available to each and every one of us through our relationship with Christ.

When we are willing to believe, we seek to understand. And when we seek to understand, we look to God's Word for that understanding. When we move through this progression, we begin to discern what pleases God, and as we discover what pleases him, we begin to want it more and more. The more we immerse ourselves in Scripture, which is one way that we abide in Christ (by hearing his voice,) the more we will find an abundance of fruit where there used to be a barren tree.

Find Out What Pleases God

In the desire for the "fruit of the Spirit" goodness, we must first and foremost abide in Christ. But understanding what that means practically can be difficult. So in order to help those of us who aren't sure what that really entails, let me start by saying that it involves finding out what pleases God. In Ephesians 5:10 we are told to "*try to discern what is pleasing to the Lord.*" And we gain this great insight into bearing fruit when Paul writes, "*And so, from the day we heard, we have not ceased to pray for you, asking that you may be filled with the knowledge of his will in all spiritual wisdom and understanding, so as to walk in a manner worthy of the Lord, fully pleasing to him, bearing fruit in every good work and increasing in the knowledge of God*" (Col. 1:9–10). Notice that Paul's prayer for the Colossians is that they would be filled with the knowledge of his will so that they would bear fruit in every good work. And it's through this knowing of God and his will that we can imitate him and, thus, grow more goodness in our lives.

Renew Your Mind

Second, in order to abide and so grow in goodness, we must consider the words of Romans 12:2: "*Do not be conformed to this world, but be transformed by the renewal of your mind, that by testing you may discern what is the will of God, what is good and acceptable and perfect.*" Renewing your mind has to do with breaking your old way of thinking and rethinking things in light of God's Word. This daily testing of your thoughts to see if they are consistent with God's Word is essential for a life bent on loving and serving God. So it may be that at first you have to stop yourself in the area of gossip and jealousy, or fear and worry, but then over time, those new patterns of thought that are in keeping with Scripture become increasingly ingrained in your soul. Then new sins pop up, and the job of renewing your mind starts over again, only in a different area. The job is never completely done, but with this constant mindfulness, prayer, and God's grace it becomes less cumbersome and more second nature. And the result is always more fruit in keeping with doing what is good and acceptable and perfect in God's sight.

Practice Thankfulness

Expressing thanksgiving can seem like a lie when things are tough. When the pain sears and the memories burn, being thankful seems counterintuitive, but giving thanks pleases God. Psalm 92:1 says that *"it is good to give thanks to the LORD, to sing praises to your name, O Most High."* Goodness is displayed in giving thanks because it acknowledges God's goodness in our lives, no matter what the circumstances. Can you thank God for everything, even the bad things? When you can, then giving thanks to the man in your life, even when he doesn't do exactly what you want, or he does exactly what you hate, is easier, because it is God whom you are ultimately thanking as the giver of life. As we read in Lamentations 3:38, it is from *"the Most High that good and bad come."* So goodness expresses thankfulness, because goodness sees the hand of God in every situation.

Draw Near to God

Life is busy for all of us, so busy that we often fail to make time to sit down and devote ourselves to God. But in the words of the psalmist, *"It is good to be near God; I have made the Lord GOD my refuge, that I may tell of all your works"* (Ps. 73:28). Goodness is exhibited by devotion. As we make God our refuge and draw near to him, the fruit of the Spirit grows.

Love God's Precepts

A lot can be said in the negative about the law. Yet in Psalm 119:39–40 we read that God's law is good, and that great men of God long for his precepts. Why can we say this with such confidence, when we know we are saved by grace and not by works? (see Eph. 2:8). Because this isn't a conversation about salvation but about goodness, and the goodness in us responds to the goodness of God. God, in his goodness, found it good to give us laws, rules, and precepts in order that we might live in love and recognize what is good and pleasing to him, regardless of our ability or inability in the flesh to keep them.

Confess Your Failure to Others

There is much sin in our lives, but God's plan provides not only for forgiveness from that sin but also for healing from it. **The Holy Spirit encourages transparency.** In fact, the only truly transparent person is one who is filled with the Holy Spirit. Because in God there is no darkness, the Spirit urges us to turn on the lights through confessing to others. In James 5:16 we read this: "*Therefore, confess your sins to one another and pray for one another, that you may be healed. The prayer of a righteous person has great power as it is working.*" **Confessing your sins to one another is an important part of healing from those sins. When we are transparent about our sin, we loosen its grip on our lives.** Sin kept private has great power, but sin brought out in public is weak and anemic and eventually dies from exposure to God's Word and to the prayer of God's people. Goodness flourishes in the light, so bring your sins out into the light so that God's truth might shine within you.

Live in Unity

The Holy Spirit creates unity. God deems it so essential that he sent his only Son to die for us so that he could restore our unity with him through reconciliation. And he wants the same for his children in relationship·with others. In Psalm 133:1 we see *"how good and pleasant it is when brothers dwell in unity!"* So the Spirit reveals himself in your marriage when you can live in unity with your husband. This means that you will not be at odds with him, rebellious, vindictive, argumentative, or silent, because all those things destroy the unity of the Spirit. It also means that the fruitful woman does not contradict her husband either to her children or to her friends. Unity demands harmony and cooperation. And unity is something that God considers good for you.

Encourage Him

In 1 Thessalonians 5:11 we are commanded to *"encourage one another and to build one another up."* This means that we are to be vigilant about reminding one another of what we already know about faith and God, helping each other to remain alert and aware of our sins and leading us to repentance. We are called to build one another up, that is, to seek the good of one another and not just please ourselves, as is seen in 1 Corinthians 10:23: *"'All things are lawful,' but not all things are helpful. 'All things are lawful,' but not all things build up."* Part of this is as simple as giving a helping hand rather than the backhand of judgment or disgrace. Goodness looks for edification, not destruction. It builds up; it doesn't tear down.

Intercede

With intercession God is well pleased. There was a time when I believed that intercession was something for those people I called "intercessors." But in 1 Timothy 2:1–4 he makes it more universal: "*I urge that supplications, prayers, interces-sions, and thanksgivings be made for all people, for kings and all who are in high positions, that we may lead a peaceful and quiet life, godly and dignified in every way. This is good, and it is pleasing in the sight of God our Savior, who desires all people to be saved and to come to the knowledge of the truth.*"

I have put intercession to the test and have found that it is life changing. Rather than bullying my way into my husband's spiritual life and making demands based on what I would do, I pray for him. I can tell you for certain that we cannot change anyone, especially our husband! But God is in the business of change. The woman who turns her concerns and her ques-tions over to God finds more change than she could ever have dreamed of. Sometimes in her husband. Many times within herself.

Every time there has been something in Michael that I wanted changed, something that I knew God saw and believed was unhappy with as well, I have gone not to Michael but to God. At the end of our spats, I go directly to my prayer closet and talk to God about it. Every time that I have seen something in Michael's life or in our marriage that has needed growth or change and have prayed about it, I have seen change—some-times immediate, sometimes gradual. Many times the change is within me. But every time, it's miraculous, truly. Intercession is good because God wants us to bring all our concerns to him rather than focus on our problems and ourselves. He wants us to love others and serve them and do all we can to minister to them, and one way we do this is through prayer.

* * *

Goodness is a natural and obvious outflowing of the life lived in Christ. As you begin to focus on him and his perfect will, you will begin to see goodness as a supernatural part of your life. But if that hasn't been the case so far, you cannot consider progress impossible. Maybe it has just been that you have not set your mind on the things of the Spirit, but now that you are, now that you've been made aware, things will begin to change. After all, we know from reading Ephesians 2:10 that *"we are his workmanship, created in Christ Jesus for good works, which God prepared beforehand, that we should walk in them."* This specific promise for goodness is your guarantee. You have all within you that you need in Christ. Trust that he is enough and see your life go from bad to good in the sweetest blink of an eye.

But the fruit of the Spirit is
FAITHFULNESS

FAITHFULNESS

I do not pray for success. I ask for faithfulness.

—MOTHER TERESA

*Men become unfaithful out of desire, fear,
weakness, loss of interest, or because of
some strong influence from without.*

—A. W. TOZER

Imagine a world without faithfulness, a world where no one would make an agreement unless it was immediately fulfilled, where no one would trust a physician, or a friend. Imagine a world where no one was faithful, where no trust could be had. Now imagine what that would do to the people who lived there. It would isolate them, tear them up, send them into arguments, battles, and war. It would destroy any sense of community or love, because without faithfulness there is no one you could have faith in, and without faith we'd all have to look out for ourselves, because no one else could be trusted. Every man would be considered a liar, no alliances would be built, no love shared, and no hope would be had. Nations would crumble, anarchy would reign. And the survival of the fittest would be the law.

Unfaithfulness is not a minor violation but major rebellion against the laws of God set down in order to ensure the survival of society, community, and love. Of all the fruit of the Spirit, faithfulness seems to be the easiest to claim. The last thing I want to do is call myself a liar or say that I can't be trusted. When my integrity is questioned, my flesh immediately wants to defend myself. I think most people can relate.

Deep down we all intrinsically understand the importance of our word, of the faith others have in us, so who would claim to be deceptive and unfaithful?

One of the most emotionally painful things in the world is finding out you've been deceived. We all can probably tell some story about being lied to. In fact, most of us have probably vowed never to let another person deceive us again. Finding out that someone you love has lied to you is one of the most devastating things that can happen in a relationship.

Before I met my husband, he was living a lie. His life, after college, had gone from bad to worse. And he found himself trading normalcy for addiction. In order to cope with the strain of it all, he had turned to a hidden addiction, gambling. No one knew what he was doing, where he was going, or how bad it was getting; no one knew the dark side of his life. But no one wins forever. Since he began to run out of money but still needed the rush of the game, he decided to "borrow" money from his place of work. He would gamble the cash he took from the petty cash box and then return it when he had made enough back to cover his "loan." But a place of business doesn't take too well to "borrowing," especially when it's a public institution. So when his addiction was found out, he was fired and taken to jail.

But this wasn't the end of the story; it was the beginning. This is where his life finally turned around, and where he turned his life over to Christ. A few years later we met, and the first thing he did on our first date was to tell me the whole sordid story. He didn't leave anything out. He wanted me to know exactly what I was getting into, so he brought everything out into the light.

Years later, while the two of us were talking on *Family Life Today* with Dennis Rainey and Bob Lepine, Dennis asked me how I could trust Michael after hearing his story. He wondered if his financial unfaithfulness in his past gave me any fear about his future faithfulness. I had never been asked that before, but I had a quick answer. "I have no fear at all," I said. Their eyes grew bigger; after all, how could I be so naive, really, to have no fear of Michael's addiction after his years of deception? The answer was easy: "Because he was so transparent about his sin. He didn't hide anything." A deceiver hides his deception, protects it. But Michael brought it out into the light for all to see, on our first date no less, and that revealed his faithfulness to me like nothing else could have.

You've Gotta Have Faith

What we first know about faithfulness is found in the character of God. His faithfulness is our measure and the requirement of our faith. It is an obvious fruit of the Spirit, because it is the essence of the Spirit. Without faithfulness God would not be God. He is by definition faithful, trustworthy, and reliable. Therefore, those who live by his Spirit must be the same. Because God is perfect—perfectly good, perfectly kind, perfectly omniscient, and perfectly omnipotent—he must be perfectly reliable. If he were unfaithful, then it would mean he wasn't perfectly perfect, and to have faith in him would be insanity. **His faithfulness is essential to our faith, and it leads to our faithfulness.**

In marriage relationships faithfulness is most often thought of as having a spouse that doesn't cheat. But faithfulness isn't just about emotional and sexual fidelity in marriage; it's that, plus a whole lot more. At its root faithfulness is about trustworthiness and reliability. The faithful do what they say they will do, and you can trust their words to be true. You can rely on them because they don't promise and then abandon their promises.

Faithfulness Does What Is True

In marriage, **faithfulness isn't a steadfast devotion to your spouse, but to your God.** Faithfulness finds its fullness in who

God is and not in whom you married. The devotion that one person has for another is grounded in his or her commitment to the covenant of marriage.

A few years ago Michael and I counseled a couple in crisis. They came to us separately to ask us to help them decide the next steps in a marriage that had fallen apart due to the husband's unfaithfulness. For the past few years this man had been involved in over dozens of extramarital affairs with different women. He had lied, cheated, and broken all the vows of marriage, and his wife had finally found out the truth. As the wife sat across from me and cried, I was grieved, but I was also comforted and inspired by the faithfulness of God. So with great certainty I told her that this was not the end and that faithfulness and love could be restored. Her husband was contrite about his promiscuity and wanted to end it. He wasn't hiding anything or arguing his case; he was coming to her asking to work things out, so we set about restoration and reconciliation between the two.

For the next six months we met with the couple, both together and individually, and by the end of that time they were like newlyweds, devoted to each other and to God more than they ever had been before. This tragedy, it turns out, was used for the betterment of their souls. What looked like the destruction of a family was really a new beginning.

I bring up this story of unfaithfulness to better explain the evidence of faithfulness that is so important. Faithfulness walks in the light. **It is only unfaithfulness that hides in darkness.** Once the husband's sin was willingly brought into the light, his faithfulness was born. In John 3:21 we read that *"whoever does what is true comes to the light, so that it may be clearly seen that his works have been carried out in God."* So faithfulness is never deceptive. It doesn't hide in the dark and cover up sin, but agrees with God and comes out into the open and confesses sin without fear or embarrassment.

Faithfulness Agrees with God

But **unfaithfulness isn't always hidden.** There are many who are proud of their unfaithfulness and even flaunt it. This showing off of sin isn't the same as bringing it into the light. The light doesn't refer to the light of day or to a lamp that makes it physically visible to everyone around, but to the light of God. In 1 John 1:5 we learn that *"God is light, and in him is no darkness at all."* So those who live in the light live as God commands. Darkness isn't really about deception, then, but about the absence of faithfulness to God's Word. First John 1:6–8 goes on to put it this way: *"If we say we have fellowship with him while we walk in darkness, we lie and do not practice the truth. But if we walk in the light, as he is in the light, we have fellowship with one another, and the blood of Jesus his Son cleanses us from all sin. If we say we have no sin, we deceive ourselves, and the truth is not in us."* **So it is our transparency, our ability to admit our sin and to continually apply God's Word to our lives, that enables us to walk in the light and so demonstrates Christ in us.**

Faithfulness Isn't Self-Deceptive

Self-deception is a common condition among women. We live in the lies that bring us comfort, allow us to maintain some semblance of control, or protect us from the world. These lies we tell ourselves promise to benefit us, preaching peace and power, but in the end they lead only to destruction. For example, many women believe that there is nothing wrong with talking a lot. I know of which I speak; I love to talk, and it seems harmless enough, but God's Word wants us to guard our mouths. In Proverbs 13:3 we read that *"whoever guards his mouth preserves his life; he who opens wide his lips comes to ruin."* This self-deception brought on by our desire to be heard can lead to a terrible thing, a worthless religion, filled with pride, complaint, gossip, and criticism.

In other words, **self-deception leads to unfaithfulness**, or a lack of trustworthiness and obedience to God's Word. Faithfulness requires truth telling, it requires that we be honest with ourselves about our motives and our actions. It requires that we be honest about our sin and our propensity to want life to be all about us. Faithfulness isn't just about not cheating on someone but about living a life of truth in our depths—truth that permeates all of our thoughts, words, and actions. We aren't going to be perfect, but we are going to pursue truth rather than relish our blissful ignorance of our own shortcomings and sin.

Faithfulness Doesn't Exaggerate

Exaggeration is a natural expression in the life of faithlessness because instead of trusting the truth of God, it "improves" upon it in order to ensure success. Exaggeration may seem harmless, but in it is the first step in proving our untrustworthiness. After all, **if exaggeration adds to the truth in order to make it more appealing, then the exaggerator doesn't covet the truth as much as she thinks she does. A half-truth is a whole lie.**

CONFESSIONS OF AN EXAGGERATOR. I am well versed in the art of exaggeration and embellishment. For years people disliked my use of the words *you always* or *I never.* When they would balk at my strong statements, I would say they were being too difficult. I was, after all, only using these extreme statements to prove a point. Whether they were true or not didn't matter to me. If I could make a point more soundly by making categorical statements or exaggerating something, then I would do it. And many years passed before I considered this to be not just a lie but a self-obsessed effort to deceive another so that I could win the argument, make the case, or get the laugh. It was all about me and my pleasurable sensations in relationship to others and not my love of faithfulness that compelled me to exaggerate.

Faithfulness Isn't Fond of Drama

When we dramatize our circumstances, we are being unfaithful. Allowing drama makes our little mess the most important thing in the world. It trumps the cross and God's grace. It magnifies the ills of the day, and the sin against us seems unforgivable. **It is in our moments of unfaithfulness that we overreact to the mistakes, shortcomings, and sins of our loved ones.** Certainly their unfaithfulness may be evident, but that doesn't give us the right to join in the chorus of sin. Overreacting to the bad things in life can keep us stuck in the mire of unfaithfulness.

Drama draws attention to our self-righteousness and away from Christ's true righteousness. A woman who dramatizes her circumstances is untrustworthy because she listens not to the voice of the Holy Spirit but to her flesh, which screams to be noticed. The fruit of faithfulness can only grow from the Spirit who lives in us as we set our minds on the things of the Spirit rather than on ourselves. Faithfulness is absent of drama because it is focused on the Rock himself, who is never shaken or stirred by circumstances.

Faithfulness Isn't Unreliable

To be reliable is to be trustworthy, but when what you say isn't always what you do, it is hard for others to put their faith in you. So, how can we become reliable and live faithful lives? The reliable woman manages her time and her tongue. In other words, when she says yes to something, she is aware of her schedule and her ability to keep her commitments. The reliable are those whom others are comfortable with because they know they aren't in danger of being forgotten at the airport, canceled on at the last minute, or failed by their mismanagement of time or mind space. The reliable wife has her husband's confidence because she has proven herself faithful, even in the small things. Being unreliable might not seem like a big deal, especially when your plate is full, but we all have to remember that faithfulness is the foundation for relationships. If we can't be trusted, we aren't loving others the way God loves us.

Faithfulness Isn't Hypocritical

Hypocrisy is a glaring problem in the church today. People see Christians saying one thing and doing another. And while none of us would name ourselves hypocrites, that is what we do when we separate our faith life from our everyday life in any small portion. Therefore, we are all hypocrites to varying degrees.

Recent studies tell us that a large percentage of young people leave the church in the few years that follow high school, and I believe much of the reason is the hypocrisy they see in the church and in the lives of the people around them, especially their parents. When they see them acting one way at church and a completely different way at home, they see through the charade. So then, why would they believe in a God who seems to be so unimportant to the ones they love?

So it is with all of those around us. Our faithfulness in all things, at all times, demonstrates God's faithfulness; in fact, it may reveal his existence to those around us. Faithfulness is the opposite of hypocrisy because faithfulness believes that God has given us all that is needed for a godly life (2 Pet. 1:3). So we see that faithfulness does what is true (John 3:21), practices truth (1 John 1:6), delights in the truth (Ps. 51:6), and refuses to live a lie. In fact, in the Old Testament *truth* is a synonym for *faithfulness*. God is insistent that we all live in the truth. We know this about him because of Isaiah 45:19: "*I did not speak in secret, in a land of darkness; I did not say to the offspring of Jacob, 'Seek me in vain.' I the LORD speak the truth; I declare what is right.*" If the Holy Spirit animates the life of the believer, then the believer will live in this same truth.

Why Are We Unfaithful?

In the beginning, our first parents had a problem with faithfulness, and ever since then we've all dabbled in it from time to time, but there are none of us who are exempt from unfaithfulness. It is a part of the sin we share with Adam and Eve. In the garden, the happy couple had only one thing to do to remain faithful, one act of faithfulness that proved their loyalty and devotion to the Father, and that was to not eat from the tree of the knowledge of good and evil. But even this one demonstration of devotion proved too much for them, and so our history is written in unfaithfulness. Their lack of faithfulness from the beginning of time betrayed their fear of commitment to God. The first people to enter into relationship with God couldn't handle the commitment that relationship demanded, and so they caved. And for their children the same is still true. Our fear of commitment is one reason for our faithlessness.

This is most obviously seen in the life of an adulterer who so clearly reveals his fear in the form of tasting the apple from a forbidden tree, as did our first parents. His fear of commitment to one woman may be said to drive him to another. But he's not the only commitment-phobe. Those of us who can't commit fully to trusting God with our relationships, our schedules, and our lives reveal our own sort of fear of commitment that leaves us faithless, and so unfaithful.

I understand the hesitation and fear that come with doubt in the sovereignty and goodness of God. For many years I had a real fear of the commitment of marriage. I avoided the institution for decades before diving in. This fear of commitment made me dangerous to the men in my life. I couldn't be trusted, certainly not for the long haul, because I feared so much. And so I broke a few hearts before I finally vowed to trust the Father, the maker of man.

This same fear of commitment has made me unfaithful in other areas of life as well—in regular devotion, in career path, in relationship to other women, and the list goes on. The fear of commitment feeds unfaithfulness because faithfulness requires devotion to God at the exclusion of my own desires, wants, and needs. Faithfulness requires the death to self that Jesus so often talked about. It requires fearlessness in the face of emotional danger, of which I am not a fan.

Our inability to commit to what or who needs our commitment leads to unfaithfulness. And behind this fear is a deeper and darker root, which many in today's church fail to speak about. This archaic concept feels out of date and uncivilized or at least uneducated, but that doesn't keep it from taking place. I am talking about idolatry. Idolatry, the worship of anything or anyone other than God, is the root cause of all unfaithfulness. Idolatry happens when we go to something or someone for the things we should go to God for. When we look for comfort, peace, hope, counsel, control, joy, rest, faith, or acceptance in the arms of anything or anyone other than God, we become unfaithful, because we immediately stop serving the faithful One and start serving either sinful man or sinful self. When our ultimate satisfaction is the deciding factor in the things we do or don't do, unfaithfulness is just around the corner, because unfaithfulness takes it commands from the self-life. And the self-life is always opposed to the life of the Holy Spirit within us. In his book *The Master's Indwelling*, Andrew Murray writes, "The reason why Christians pray and pray for the Christ life to come in to them, without result, is that the self-life is not denied."[11] So it is this self-life, leading to idolatry, that keeps us in a continual battle for faithfulness.

But when your faithfulness is found in the person of Christ, when we are first and foremost devoted, loyal, and faithful to him, then we will find our allegiances to anyone or anything else broken. When this happens, then our true faithfulness will flourish, and those around us will be the beneficiaries. **A woman cannot be faithful to her man if she serves him over her Savior, and if she makes of him an idol she will surely become locked in some area of unfaithfulness, because man was never meant to take the place of God.** But when she devotes herself to Christ, her faithfulness to her husband and to others is the natural fruit of his Spirit that will be present all her life.

Finding Faithfulness

Faithfulness relies not on ourselves but on God. As hard as we try to be faithful, as much as we may claim our devotion, there is only one faithfulness that is assured, and that is God's faithfulness to us. During the Dark Ages many believers were torturously put to death for their faith. All they had to do was renounce their devotion to God and they would be saved from the pain of burning, beheading, or boiling in hot oil. But for centuries men and women remained faithful to God because their faithfulness was not found in their own personal strength or safety but in the one in whom they had faith.

In the year 202, this was seen beautifully and tragically in the life of a young woman named Perpetua. Thrown into prison, she was told that if she would just recant her faith then she would be set free. She refused. When her father brought her child to her and asked her to recant in order to be with her baby, she still refused. As she was hauled off with the other Christians, she knew her life was in God's hands. She was put into an arena to be hunted and killed by an angry heifer. After it gored her almost to death, she crept to the aid of one of her companions. But soon a scared young man came with sword in hand to kill her, and as he did she gently guided his hand to her throat. **Faithfulness is oftentimes the seed of belief for the faithless.** And this day the seed took root as the chief jailer, Pudens, committed himself to Christ. Perpetua's faithfulness, even at the expense of her earthly family, served the purpose of faith.[12]

It must be understood that any attempt to grow the fruit of the Spirit faithfulness is found only in union with Christ, in whom we have faith. It is his faithfulness that makes our faithfulness possible. And it is through the sap of the Holy Spirit that the power for faithfulness flows from the vine to the branch. In his strength we remain mindful of the Spirit, his will, and his ways. So before we end this chapter, let's take a look at some of the ways God wants his children to show their faithfulness to one another in everyday life.

Guard Your Tongue

It is decidedly unfaithful to share your husband's sins, failings, or emotional life with other people. When he hurts you, or you hurt for him, the flesh really wants to talk to someone about it, to get another's opinion, to vent, or to prove yourself right and him wrong. But the Spirit wants something completely different. The Spirit redirects the heart to thoughts of God rather than self, and in so doing the need to vent disappears and trust is maintained. Confession is a good thing, but each woman must confess her own sins, and not her husband's, unless he has given her permission to do so. Michael and I freely share one another's sins with others to serve as example and encouragement but never in order to serve ourselves. This must be the first rule in speech; may it always serve others over self.

When we speak with the Spirit in mind, our words give encouragement, hope, thanks, appreciation, and praise, not criticism, complaint, or discontent. When a woman is discontent, it shows her unfaithfulness to the one through whom all things come, God the Father (Lam. 3:38). Anything that comes from our mouths that accuses God of unfaithfulness, either in our marriage or in any other part of our lives, is unfaithful.

All our speech must be used to glorify God, to express his faithfulness and our love. When this is the case, your husband will find your speech to be faithful.

Support Him

And faithfulness includes support. It can be hard to support a man you disagree with, but when your goal is to glorify Christ rather than to be right, you are able to support him regardless of agreement. The Holy Spirit teaches the faithful wife to offer a support that refuses to nag, control, or micromanage her husband.

A few years ago Michael came up with a concept for a line of books called "God Girl" and "God Guy," and I thought he was crazy. I didn't like the title or the idea, but in support of him and his leadership in our business I went along with it. Rather than argue with him or attempt to prove him wrong, we wrote the books plus two devotionals to go with them, and three years later all four of them hit the Christian bestseller list. Imagine if I had chosen not to support him and instead to fight for what I wanted. There wouldn't be a GodGirl.com or GodGuy.com right now, where we're helping thousands of young men and women across the world with discipleship and mentoring. And there wouldn't be God Girl and God Guy devotional Bibles. It shouldn't have taken me so long to support him. I was hard to convince, but over the past few years I've learned that the most faithful response I can give him is my support for his ideas, even if I should disagree with them.

Control Your Spending

Finance is another area where in many cases the fruit of faithfulness finds growth no thanks to our flesh but to his Spirit. It is no secret that many women love to shop, and many of us are even addicted to the feeling of purchasing new stuff. The love affair that we have with stuff betrays our idolatry of the comfort, safety, and joy that stuff brings us. It reveals the unfaithfulness of our hearts toward our partners in this life who work so hard for us or alongside of us. But as the Spirit nourishes the fruit of faithfulness, we learn to control frivolous spending and honor our husband by living within the agreed-upon budget. To overspend and to leave him in financial turmoil is to betray his faith in you.

Avoid Emotional Affairs

In the world of social media, this might seem obvious, but it is decidedly unfaithful for anyone to have extensive online conversations with someone of the opposite sex to whom they aren't married. This kind of emotional unfaithfulness is really easy to fall into when we turn away from the matters of the Spirit to take a quick look for old flames and friends on social media sites. And while your motivation might not be adultery, the opportunity for straying, if only emotionally, is tremendous. Women bond through communicating, and to communicate intimately with those of the opposite sex is to bond with them in a way you were only meant to bond with one man, your husband. **Faithfulness puts more value in honoring God and the covenant of marriage than in curiosity or fun.**

Don't Retaliate

It is said that men tend to be unfaithful more than women. The question for women is, what happens when a man is unfaithful? Does his unfaithfulness give her permission to be unfaithful within marriage? By no means! **Another's sin is never an excuse for ours, as sin is inexcusable.** When a man is unfaithful, the faithful wife has a few options at her disposal. Either she can forgive her husband and work toward reconciliation, or she can abandon the marriage and divorce him, as infidelity and abandonment are the only biblically acceptable reasons for divorce. But consider the faithfulness that clings to God and determines to die to self in order to reconcile the relationship, especially when children are involved.

Those who say that divorce doesn't hurt the children are lying to themselves; divorce destroys the hearts of children. Ask any child of divorce, and she will agree. The levels on which divorce attacks them emotionally and psychologically are incalculable. In every marriage, there are two sinful people coming together. I'm not saying that every single marriage can be restored, but in one where the cheater is willing to submit to the counsel of Scripture, to not seek reconciliation is to miss out on a redeeming work that can testify to the world of God's grace and faithfulness.

When children are involved, I encourage all couples to go to the depths of self-death in order to restore the marriage and save the children years of emotional turmoil and suffering. Unfortunately, in many marriages where the victim agrees to "make it work" under her own power, the marriage ends up bleeding out under the death of a thousand cuts of unfaithfulness. When it comes to restoring a broken marriage, forgiveness must be given, or the marriage will not last. As I was working on this chapter, I spoke to my husband about the topic of faithfulness, and with a sad expression he began to talk about his own unfaithfulness, not in the area of sexual immorality but in the millions of smaller things: not keeping up with the yard, home repair, the bills, etc. He was remorseful, forthcoming, transparent, and contrite for his unfaithfulness, but I was quick to cheerfully forgive. After all, God does not keep a record of the wrongs of his children, so why, since we have been forgiven by God for all our sin, would we withhold the grace and faithfulness that God has so generously shared with us? The "fruit of the Spirit" faithfulness allows us to repeatedly forget, day by day, the little acts of unfaithfulness in our husband, while amplifying all the faithful things he does.

* * *

The faithful wife is a blessing to her husband because she is a safe haven for him. She can be trusted to hold her tongue and not to speak unkindly about him, to complain about him, or in any way to slander him. She can be trusted to love him without reserve, to forgive as she has been forgiven, and to do what she says she will do. Faithfulness is the bedrock of faith; without the faithfulness of our God, our faithfulness would not be possible. And without faithfulness, none of the other fruit of the Spirit would be possible. Faithfulness is more than not cheating on your husband; it is about not cheating on God by letting sin or idols become acceptable in our lives. But faithfulness cannot be sustained if it does not come from the life of the Holy Spirit within us. In order to find true faithfulness, we must crush our fear of commitment and our love of idols and choose to serve God, and God alone, no matter what the cost. When we do this, our faithfulness will shine like the noonday sun, and our God will be glorified.

But the fruit of the Spirit is
GENTLENESS

8 GENTLENESS

*Too often we sigh and look within; Jesus sighed
and looked without. We sigh, and look down; Jesus
sighed, and looked up. We sigh, and look to earth;
Jesus sighed, and looked to Heaven. We sigh, and
look to man; Jesus sighed, and looked to God.*

—THEOPHILUS STORK

*Gentleness or meekness is the opposite of self-
assertiveness and self-interest. It stems from trust
in God's goodness and control over the situation.
The gentle person is not occupied with self at all.*

—STRONG'S CONCORDANCE

Gentleness does not come naturally to me. Brutal honesty is
much more in my wheelhouse. I've never been one to tread
lightly or to be mild in personality. I've always been opinion-
ated and boisterous and considered gentleness to be reserved
for a few gifted women who, through some natural-born
favor, were made gentle for a very specific purpose, which I
would never serve. For me, gentleness was actually a disabil-
ity. It got in the way of my telling people they were complete
idiots, of calling them on their sin, of proving them wrong,
and of showing them how cool I was.

This confession is hard to write, but it must be written.
For years I walked through life like a bull in a china shop,
leaving broken hearts and shattered emotions behind me.
When people would come to me for spiritual advice, I would
quickly open them up for major surgery with the skill of a
savage rather than of a surgeon. Anesthesia was for sissies.
I can remember telling one friend who wanted me to stop

correcting her that I couldn't be her friend because there was too much I needed to correct about her. Ugh! Can you imagine? I could tell stories like these for pages. I am by nature the very opposite of gentle. I am harsh, intrusive, and loud.

So how can I come to write this chapter on the "fruit of the Spirit" gentleness? How can I speak of such a thing that comes so unnaturally to me? I can because the Holy Spirit is rewriting my DNA; he is changing me from a harsh, obnoxious soul, to a more gentle and quiet one. This gentleness that I am inheriting from my Savior is completely changing my life, and I hope that it will change yours as well. So take a look with me at the fruit of gentleness, and see what it might do for your life and marriage.

What Is Gentleness?

The "fruit of the Spirit" gentleness comes from the Greek word *prautes* (prah-ot'-ace), which refers first to your relationship with God. A gentle spirit doesn't accuse God, fight with him, or complain about the things he has allowed. How many times do we complain about life without considering that nothing happens that he doesn't allow? And so we accuse God, even blame him, for our miserable condition. But **as the fruit of gentleness grows in our lives, a sense of calm comes over us, and we are less likely to disdain the circumstances in which we live.** Gentleness refers to an easiness, a carefreeness that reveals a heart that is in meekness set on nothing but the will of the Father. When your heart is there, nothing can hurt or derail your life, because everything that happens is in his will or it wouldn't have come to pass. After all, John 3:27 tells us that "*a person cannot receive even one thing unless it is given him from heaven.*" A gentle woman understands this and is therefore free to trust God even when the pain is too much to bear.

Nowhere is this seen so beautifully as in the garden of Gethsemane, where Christ went to plead the anguish of his heart with the Father in true gentleness by saying, *"My Father, if this cannot pass unless I drink it, your will be done"* (see Matt. 26:39). Surely Christ had the power to stop the crucifixion, or to avoid it or interrupt it, but in the spirit of *prautes*, he did not. He gently and humbly accepted the Father's will. Here is where we begin to dive into the depths of *prautes*, as we see how it manifests itself in the life of Christ.

Meekness isn't an often-used term in modern English. In fact, it kind of leaves you with a bad taste in your mouth when you say it. In English, the word brings to mind the idea of its rhyming cousin *weakness*, an inability to do anything for yourself, a church mouse, a doormat, a wimp. But in the Greek there is no taste of weakness in meekness. It is more correct to say that meekness is "strength and courage under control, coupled with kindness."[13] Christ was never weak; he was never a wimp, never a victim, yet he is described as meek. In fact, he describes himself this way when he says, *"Take my yoke upon you, and learn from me, for I am gentle and lowly in heart, and you will find rest for your souls"* (Matt. 11:29). The soul that is gentle rests in the knowledge that God has everything under control and that nothing is outside of his sight or righteousness. It is best described as a calmness of spirit "that is neither elated nor cast down, simply because it is not occupied with self at all."[14]

But as the fruit of the Spirit serves to feed those around us, so this *prautes* serves to feed more than our souls. As it assures us that we can have complete and absolute dependence on God for everything in our lives, it changes our feelings and actions toward others. **Gentleness, then, lives out of our certainty that this isn't our world, but God's, and because of that there is nothing in it that we must manipulate or control.** So it is in gentleness that we react to the people in our lives and feed them the fruit of the Spirit that will not only nourish them, but also point them back to the vine from which it grows.

But what does this gentleness, grounded in meekness, look like in everyday life? It is first important to make this distinction: **meekness, also called "humility," is the foundation of all righteousness,** because it is in humility that we can place absolute dependence on God for everything that we need. Without meekness or the humility to admit that we are nothing and God is everything, there would be no confession, no repentance, and no salvation. The converse is also true—**pride is the foundation of all sin.** So it isn't at all ironic that God would list as fruit of the Spirit this gentleness, or meekness of *prautes*, as a characteristic of a life filled with and led by the power of the Holy Spirit.

In understanding what gentleness looks like, we need only take a look at the difference between pride and humility. When we walk humbly, as Christ did, we will display the fruit of gentleness to those around us. This humility manifests itself with an "ungrudging and unhypocritical acknowledgment of absolute dependence upon God," rather than self.[15] Therefore, humility is not bent on self-protection or self-assertion. It doesn't lead us to self-indulgence or self-satisfaction. When we look out for self over God, when we consider our needs over his will, then gentleness turns to rebellion. In these moments, however mild they may seem, we are more prone to harshness, to unreasonableness, rudeness, and criticism, than to meekness and gentleness.

Gentleness speaks to our meekness before God while the opposite speaks to our pride, and our arrogance. This overwhelming drive to be the master of our own domains, to teach others in a spirit of disdain and judgment, to be quick to snap at their faults and weaknesses, and to disregard their feelings and deem our feelings as more important than theirs, rejects the gentleness of Christ and claims the pride of the world. While gentleness doesn't exclude correction, it does demand a kindness in delivery that allows the corrected to hear not our emotion but the truth of God. This is seen in Galatians 6:1, where we learn that *"if anyone is caught in any transgression, you who are spiritual should restore him in a spirit of gentleness."*

So correction, or restoration, isn't beyond the pale of gentleness, but it must be done with the meekness of spirit in mind. In the words of Oswald Chambers, it is important that we all can say, "No matter how men may treat me, they will never treat me with the spite and hatred with which I treated Jesus Christ. When we realize that Jesus Christ has served us to the end of our meanness, our selfishness, and sin, nothing that we meet with from others can exhaust our determination to serve men for His sake."[16] And there is nothing that can keep us from exercising the gentleness of the Spirit in order to serve not ourselves but God and others. So gentleness remembers what Christ has done for us and determines to do the same for others, to act not out of self-protection or self-promotion but in selflessness.

Gentleness Is Never Harsh

While we may correct others in a spirit of gentleness, we will never correct them out of anger, frustration, bitterness, or hatred. It is like they say about disciplining a child: never do it when you're angry, because it is when you act on your emotion that you act for yourself and not for truth. **When strong emotions are acted on in disagreement with Christ's gentle and meek nature, the fruit of the Spirit is choked and the flesh is fed.** But gentleness is never harsh; it is always polite, courteous, and reasonable, showing compassion and even lenience (1 Cor. 4:21; Eph. 4:2; Titus 3:2).

There have been times when I have seen mothers treating their disobedient children harshly. I ask myself how I would react to this disobedience if I were her. How would I act in gentleness in the same situation? How would I discipline as God disciplines me? The first place we must walk in the gentleness of Christ is in our closest relationships. It's so easy, out of fatigue, frustration, and anger, to lose all gentleness when the heat gets turned up on our lives, but these are just the moments when gentleness is called for. Gentleness refuses to be provoked but is reasonable in nature (Phil. 4:5). This reasonableness, as opposed to unfairness, and overreaction, reveals the Holy Spirit of God, who himself is gentle with our disobedience through his grace (Ps. 18:35).

Most people would probably say that harshness is the opposite of gentleness. Something or someone harsh is jarring to the senses, unreasonably rough, cruel, and even severe. When we **jar people or are rough with them or cruel in our approach, we reject gentleness in favor of ourselves.** This self-obsession rather than Spirit-obsession points only to our pride and our desire to be God in the lives of others. Our flesh tends to believe we know what's best for others, so we get frustrated when others don't see it that way, and we want to scream and shake them. But to vent our frustration on those who reject our input is out of place in a life led by the Spirit.

YOU BIG DUMMY! It follows that any form of harshness, whether direct or subtle, is the opposite of gentleness. This includes sarcasm, contempt, and ridicule (Matt. 12:34–37; Eph. 5:4; James 4:11). When we, as Christian women, speak with harshness toward our husbands, mocking them and making fun of their actions, this should make our hearts hurt. When we learn that compassion and gentleness combat harshness, we can take time to listen to others before we offer advice or counsel, and then do so in gentleness, even when everything in us wants to scream, "You big dummy! Don't you see?" But as we saw in Galatians 6, restoration of those in error is to be done in a spirit of gentleness, not harshness, because harshness is inconsistent with the fruit of the Spirit.

It might look as though, when Jesus overturned the tables of the moneychangers in the temple, that he was being the opposite of gentle. However, in the temple Christ was displaying his anger against sin and its assault against the Father. Never did he fight for himself but for his Father in heaven. Jesus lashed out against an attack on the very temple of God and revealed his displeasure with sin. Gentleness is founded in meekness, the selflessness of humility that says, "Life isn't about me but about God." The Greek philosopher Aristotle was not a Christian, but he was well versed in the Greek language, so he knew better than anyone the meaning of *prautes*. With regard to this word he said that *prautes* is angry **"on the right grounds, and against the right persons, and in the right manner, and at the right moment, and for the right length of time."** How beautifully this describes the wrath of Christ in the temple while also exposing our wrongful wrath against those who frustrate or bother us.

Gentleness Is Teachable

Another important characteristic of a gentle woman is that she is teachable. How many of us have seen women who were bound and determined never to change, never to grow, and never to be told what to do? I have run into women who refuse to be taught by anyone; instead, they complain and moan about a pastor or Bible teacher who asks too much or ignore a friend who lovingly corrects or admonishes. **An unteachable spirit indicates a life led by the flesh and deaf to the Holy Spirit.** The truth is that if God isn't changing you, he hasn't saved you (2 Cor. 3:18). We are new creatures in Christ, not old ones (2 Cor. 5:17). And since no one is perfect, not even one (Rom. 3:10), we all have room for improvement. The Fruitful Wife is teachable because she is humble and gentle in spirit and has no delusion about her remaining sinfulness.

The teachable woman is a pleasure to be around. She isn't overreactive or bitter when corrected. She isn't combative or belligerent, because she is honest in her assessment of herself and in her desire to become more like Christ. She knows that everything that feels like an attack on her personality or emotions is simply a tool in the hands of God, working to pry away her sinful exterior and get her to look at the Spirit that lives inside of her. In this way her gentleness benefits both herself and others. **The woman who sees God's fingerprints on everything in the world, including insult and injury, cannot be destroyed and doesn't harbor or nurse wounds, for she knows that God's hand is far greater and his will far more important and powerful than the hands, the will, and the power of man.**

Gentleness Isn't Meddlesome

Consider the lack of gentleness in your life and your personal law as a chance to be mindful toward God's Spirit and to see if there are areas in your life where he'd like you to lighten up and to live a more gentle life. Remember that while he walked this earth, Christ didn't micromanage the lives of the people around him. He wasn't controlling in his demands of their obedience. He didn't run after the rich young ruler who wouldn't sell all he had to follow him. Jesus didn't chase him down and demand compliance. If then, being so perfect and wise, he can allow people to fail, why do we believe it to be our job to micromanage the life of our husband? Can we trust God to speak to him, teach him, and lead him just as well as he does us? Gentleness compels women to loosen up, to let their men make mistakes, and to rely on the faithfulness and wisdom of God to fix whatever mess they may make.

The same principle applies in our other relationships. Women who want to involve themselves in other people's business and attempt to fix them, change them, or somehow micromanage their lives are meddlesome, and this is not a character trait of gentleness. It is harshness that interjects itself into the lives of others uninvited, and so the fruit of the Spirit doesn't serve this end. The busybody or meddlesome woman isn't walking in quiet gentleness, but in the harshness of control and micromanaging. But gentleness allows God to do what God does best—take care of everything, be in control, and manage the lives of his children.

Gentleness Is Polite

Gentleness implies a degree of courtesy or politeness. *Politeness* is showing respect in all of your actions and words, which can often be easier to do in public than in private. We women can be sweet and polite with strangers but rude and disrespectful with our husband. We don't mean to be impolite; we are just being honest, telling him like it is, and doing what we can to fix him, teach him, and help him. And while politeness might seem like something that's reserved for acquaintances and not spouses, that is decidedly untrue. Ephesians 5:33 confirms it. After teaching men to love their wife, Paul adds, "*Let the wife see that she respects her husband*," and being polite is one indicator of that respect.

This might seem like an unnecessary discussion to many women, but to women like me who see their spouse as someone so close to us that politeness seems too formal, it's essential. It took me a long time to learn this lesson. I never said "please" or "thank you" when my husband did things around the house. Even though those words are the most obvious part of being polite, I saw no need for them when he was doing what he was supposed to do. But then I started to watch women interacting with their husband, and I started to put myself in the men's shoes, seeing how they would feel with an impolite wife, and I became sickened by my own lack of understanding and gentleness. This encouraged me to begin saying "thank you" when he did things like take out the trash, clean up after himself, or take us out to dinner. No longer did I consider him so close to me that I didn't have to be polite, but I took God's Word and applied it to my marriage. When I did, things in our household started to change. The romance of our courtship started to return, my joy came back, and our relationship got better.

It's hard for a man to be a good husband when his wife doesn't respect him. Whether the chicken or the egg comes first, I cannot say, but I do know that a man will live up to his wife's expectations of him. If she treats him impolitely, talks poorly to him, cuts him down, or isn't even as gentle with him as she is with strangers, then he's going to be reduced to her image of him. But if she treats him in a way that brings honor both to him and to God, he will soon begin to want to live up to her degree of love and respect.

Gentleness Isn't Trying to Be Perfect

Turning our attention more inward, let's take a look at the problem of perfectionism. Perfectionists often believe that their neurosis affects only themselves, that their problem is such a part of who they are that it cannot be changed. But this is not true. Perfectionism plagues more than the obsessed one; it also harms those around her. The problem with perfectionism is that it comes from a heart that believes that it deserves to be—no, must be—perfect. Perfectionists base who they are on how well they do things. In other words, they serve their pride and their sense of self through their efforts. This is pride and has no meekness in it. The meek or gentle spirit is content with things, even imperfect things. She puts no demands on herself that don't come directly from God, and she accepts his grace in those moments when she fails. "*For by grace you have been saved through faith. And this is not your own doing; it is the gift of God, not a result of works, so that no one may boast*" (Eph. 2:8–9).

The perfectionist has no time for grace, and in the path of perfectionism lies battered relationships that experience the prideful wrath of the moments when perfection fails. Gentleness carries with it a sober understanding of who we are: broken and frail, fallen and unrighteous. It agrees with God and can claim that only Christ is perfect. It doesn't, in pride, demand more of itself, as if it were better than others, but instead agrees with God that we are sinners saved by grace and unable to make ourselves perfect, no matter how hard we work. This should come as a relief to the perfectionist.

The lie that everything you do has to be perfect comes from the pit of hell. It argues with God over the true nature of your soul, sinful and broken, and it demands recognition for being, well, perfect. But gentleness makes no such demands. In peace it allows God to be all and so relies not on success or perfection to be the reward for hard work. **Gentleness is freedom for the perfectionist—forever changing the subject to the Father and forever allowing success to be defined as loving God with everything and loving others as ourselves.**

Gentleness Isn't Vengeful

Vengeance opposes gentleness. Vengeance demands pain on the part of the offender, and so any act of vengeance is a rejection of the fruit of gentleness. You might not consider yourself to be a vengeful woman, but if there was ever a time when you withheld something from your husband because he had hurt you or made your life more difficult, then vengeance was yours.

Withholding kind words or affection is a way of getting revenge. How many times have I fought with Michael and then clammed up, feeling unable to say a word out of anger, frustration, bitterness, or hurt feelings? Too many to count! It's part of our nature—we get hurt and clam up. But just because it's in our nature doesn't mean we have to obey it. Our sin nature was never meant to be obeyed but to be rejected and remade by the gospel. Gentleness rejects retaliation in favor of love and kindness, humility, and meekness. Actions governed by the flesh are a rejection of God's rule over us. "*Do not say, 'I will do to him as he has done to me; I will pay the man back for what he has done'*" (Prov. 24:29). Do not let your desire for retaliation spoil the fruit that God wants to grow in your life.

Vengeance also includes pouting, sulking, and moodiness. These actions speak to a life animated by emotion rather than by the Spirit. Emotions may run strong, but they are not meant to be obeyed. For almost three decades I was ruled by my emotions, believing whatever I felt had to be obeyed and acted upon. But then I learned this truth: "*To set the mind on the flesh is death, but to set the mind on the Spirit is life and peace. For the mind that is set on the flesh is hostile to God, for it does not submit to God's law; indeed, it cannot*" (Rom. 8:6–7). The desire to pout and sulk is destructive. In gentleness and meekness we must resist the urge to react out of the flesh and instead embrace the desires of the Spirit.

Gentleness Is Quiet

Because a wife whose life is characterized by gentleness isn't occupied with self, she isn't loud, showy, or ostentatious. An important description of a godly woman is found in 1 Peter 3:4. Peter's words here are often rejected because they are inconsistent with modern women. The words have long been a stumbling block for me, something I've tripped over repeatedly as I've walked through life, but a better understanding of their true meaning has helped me, and maybe it will help you. Peter writes, "*Let your adorning be the hidden person of the heart with the imperishable beauty of a gentle and quiet spirit, which in God's sight is very precious.*" Because the words *gentle* and *quiet* don't appeal to our modern sensibilities, we allow ourselves to think they were applicable only in an earlier time. Is God asking us to deny ourselves and to become church mice, wallflowers, or Plain Janes?

Let's start to answer that with this idea, and that is that drawing attention to ourselves is the opposite of gentleness. When I was a younger woman I often commanded a room. When I arrived, I made sure everyone knew it. I am by nature shy, but when I was with those I knew well, I was anything but. I dressed to get attention, and I was loud. But as I looked more closely at the life of Christ, I began to see a disconnect between my behavior and his. And I began to want change. It wasn't a conscious, all-at-once change, but a slow metamorphosis that brought me from loud and showy closer to happy and meek. There are times when I now feel lost in the crowd, unnoticed and unimportant. I can blend so much that no one seems to notice me, but what an improvement, because now, instead of making people notice me, I am noticing people. I am finding faces that I would have previously ignored. I am seeing pain I would have previously been oblivious to, and I am taking my mind's eye off myself and instead serving God and his children.

When we draw attention to ourselves through our loudness or personal branding, we are abrasive, not gentle and quiet. And we draw attention from God onto ourselves. This includes those moments when we are showy in our emotional life, revealing our deep elation or dejection; in both cases gentleness is removed as we bare ourselves for all to see. Gentleness, like its synonym *meekness*, leads us to restraint and mildness.

The Wisdom of Gentleness

Gentleness was, for our Savior, a part of his very nature, as it is for the Father (2 Sam. 22:36). So it is a part of our inheritance as children of God to emulate that same gentleness in our own lives. This gentleness described by Jesus as meekness in Matthew 5:5 assures that the meek shall inherit the earth. **The meek come close to the glory of God because they deny their flesh and instead insist upon the faithfulness and goodness of God.** It is in gentleness and meekness that the Fruitful Wife can respond to wounds from insults or wrong done to her and look away from her desire to control others or seek revenge.

It is in gentleness and meekness that the Fruitful Wife finds wisdom. Meekness is too often associated with weakness, but the truth is that wisdom is by its very nature meek. We know this from the words penned in James 3:13: "*Who is wise and understanding among you? By his good conduct let him show his works in the meekness of wisdom.*" This wisdom is gained through understanding, and understanding through receiving "with meekness" (James 1:21), the implanted word of God. So then, meekness, or gentleness, is essential for any of us to grow in faith and wisdom. Without meekness through the Spirit, we cannot know or understand God's Word.

And without the meekness of the believing wife, the unbelieving husband would be lost, for as we see in 1 Peter 3:1 women are called to live in gentleness and meekness with their unsaved husbands so that "*even if some do not obey the word, they, without a word, may be won by the conduct of their wives, when they observe your chaste conduct accompanied by fear*" (1 Peter 3:1–2 NKJV). This chaste conduct speaks to the gentleness and quietness mentioned later in verse 4 of this same chapter.

Living Gently

The seeds of faith are sown in your heart, but the abundance of the fruit of the Spirit that grows from them shows up in your character, actions, and words. When gentleness is a part of your life, when you refuse to give in to your emotions and to be ruled by them, you feed those around you, both believing and unbelieving, with the gentleness of God, and through you they are better able to see his face. Gentleness serves more than your relationships but it is still essential to those relationships. So now, let's take a closer look at how the Holy Spirit can enable gentleness in marriage. Each of these things that characterize gentleness will become supernaturally natural to the woman who is intent on listening for the promptings of the Spirit and moving in step with him.

Be More Easy Going

You don't find thistles or thorns growing on grapevines. They would make picking the fruit dangerous, and if our fruit is meant to nourish those around us, we can't have land mines waiting to hurt those we were meant to feed. So as fruit bearers, the Holy Spirit compels us to a **sweet temper**. Many of us weren't gifted with the sweetness that seems to come so easily to some, yet we are all called to the same gentle way. So how does the Holy Spirit teach us true sweetness in relationship to those we love?

When your husband disappoints you or does something wrong, frustrating, or even cruel, how you react to him reveals the sweetness or bitterness of your heart. Sweetness of temper is easy when life is rosy and good, but it is when things get difficult that gentleness is proven (1 Pet. 2:23). So when your husband forgets your anniversary, the Holy Spirit compels you to find no insult in it. When he says you are overspending or oversharing, the Spirit of gentleness inspires an apology rather than an excuse (Prov. 17:10).

When you respond to the Holy Spirit's sweetness of temper, your mood isn't soured by the words, actions, or moods of others. When someone hurts us, our first reaction is self-protection, and in self-protection we most often act not in gentleness but in the aggression of defense. **The thorns on the** bush are put there to protect the plant from enemies, but the fruit of the Spirit is meant for friends and enemies alike, so the thorns that grow from your flesh must be pruned away.

When we are upset at insults, when we don't want to be accommodating or sympathetic, when we demand perfection from others and bristle at their failures and sins, we reject the gentleness of Christ and opt for the harshness of the world that lives without grace. But the gentleness that flows from the Holy Spirit gives us the warmth that suffers little from the world and its failures, and in turn causes the world to suffer little from our own.

Accept Correction

When first faced with the prospect of a Christian marriage, I was literally sick thinking of the S word, *submission*. I rejected it firmly and desperately wanted to get out from under it, but I equally desperately wanted to marry Michael, so I was in a bit of a pickle. The hardest part for me wasn't being led but being seen in all my sin and being called out on it. But Michael explained to me that gentle correction isn't meant to destroy a wife but to build her up, to reveal weaknesses and sinful areas and to administer the Word of God in order to bring her into submission to God. For the woman who desires to grow in her obedience to the Spirit, then, correction can be a painful but welcome prescription for change and growth.

When a man corrects a woman who allows her life to be directed by the Spirit, something amazing happens. Her previously defensive reaction is softened, because a defensive response is a barrier to the hand of God that might work through her husband to affect the change needed to draw her closer to God himself. This is true, even when the husband is incorrect in his assessment. When it comes to being corrected, we must all remember that we submit to our husband not because he is always right, but because God is, and in God's rightness he has commanded our submission to this one man.

If we are to take God's Word seriously, we must consider that any rejection of correction, any active defiance, disrespect, or dishonor of our husband, or any failure to be gentle with him may be considered an act of rebellion against God. Since we are called to submit to our husband (Eph. 5:22), then we must do so with gentleness, and we can do so as we surrender our agenda to the will of God and his Holy Spirit within us.

Live a Modest Life

Modesty is another aspect of gentleness. Modesty doesn't apply exclusively to wardrobe but encompasses anything that would draw attention to ourselves. As we begin to be mindful of the Spirit for our choices, modesty becomes our natural bent. Modesty does its best to remove all eyes from self. When given accolades or honor, modesty deflects it upward. The nature of our flesh is to compare ourselves with others, but as we stop living for ourselves and start living for him, we stop needing to compare ourselves with others unless we're trying to make them look good. We aren't trying to win the approval of men but of God (Gal. 1:10), and so we choose not only our clothes but also our words with great thought and concern for the will of the Father.

The gentleness of the Holy Spirit also compels us to be considerate and sympathetic toward the temptations of others. He makes us aware of our surroundings. For example, if you are in the company of an alcoholic, you don't offer him a beer. And if you are in the company of a man other than your husband, you don't expose your flesh. The Holy Spirit, when responded to, compels you to think more highly of others than of yourself and so refuse to lead others to stumble.

Be Kind to Those Who Can Do Nothing for You

When people treat me as a second-class citizen, it makes me crazy. I want to ask them why they are so high and mighty. I've been to big conferences where I've spoken alongside famous Christian people who have completely ignored me, acting as if I were inconsequential to their lives and therefore not deserving of their attention. I know celebrity is the way of the world, but it should never be the way of faith. The true test of people's character is how they act toward people who can do absolutely nothing for them. Christ loved every person he interacted with while he walked this earth, even though they could do nothing for him. And his Spirit in us still finds value in every human being, not just those who can do something for us. The words of Christ should ring in all of our minds that *"whoever would be great among you must be your servant, and whoever would be first among you must be your slave"* (Matt. 20:26–27). To assume the position of first instead of last is to reject the gentleness that is meant to be ours in the Spirit.

Unstuff

Stuff is very fun. I love stuff; I can never get enough of it—so much so that I have to be careful, because stuff can quickly get the best of me, and I quickly end up buying more than I can afford and owning more than I can accommodate. My house can literally burst at the seams and still I want more stuff. But once the Holy Spirit gets ahold of the surrendered heart, this desire for stuff starts to weaken and the deaccumulation of stuff becomes our goal. The gentleness of the Spirit has no aspiration that stuff can fulfill, primarily the aspiration of being above others who have less, or at least the same amount. Gentleness is removed from worldly competitiveness and so does all it can not to battle it out with others in the area of stuff. Certainly stuff is a blessing, but when stuff becomes about showing off, impressing, or fitting in, then we have a problem. The more we depend on the Spirit to lead us, the more we have no desire to keep up with the Joneses, but instead we find fulfillment in loving the Joneses more than self and pointing them to Christ rather than the beauty and quality of our stuff.

* * *

John Bunyan called the Valley of Humiliation "the most fruitful piece of ground in all these parts," because it is in the valley of humiliation where the most abundant fruit is grown.[17] It is through the act of self-denial, humiliation, and meekness that we are able to see the biggest growth at the hand of the Holy Spirit in our lives. And it is through our acceptance of the meekness seen in the life of Christ and let into our lives that our relationships begin to flourish. Imagine a world where everyone was meek, where we all pointed upward, where we were filled with compassion, selflessness, reasonableness, and sweetness. Imagine a world filled with only gentle people who embodied the very gentle Spirit of God in all their dealings, and imagine a marriage where that was the case.

Even if your husband doesn't show you the same gentleness you show him, this shouldn't dissuade you, because through the growth of this beautiful fruit in your own life, his life may soon change. The fruit of gentleness that is born of the Spirit is a gift you can give your husband. Regardless of those around you, gentleness made real in your life will make you more and more into the image of Christ himself.

But the fruit of the Spirit is

SELF-CONTROL

9 SELF-CONTROL

*You were trusting in yourself, or you could not have
failed. If you had trusted Christ, He could not fail.*

—ANDREW MURRAY

*If Jesus ever gave us a command He could not enable
us to fulfill, He would be a liar; and if we make our
inability a barrier to obedience, it means we are telling
God there is something He has not taken into account.*

—OSWALD CHAMBERS

My name is Hayley, and I am a glutton. I am given to excess.
If something is good I want more of it. Even if my mind says,
"No more," my taste buds say, "Just one more." What I want
to do, I don't do. And what I do, I love, at least while I'm doing
it, and then when it's all done, I'm back to feeling the same way
I did before I indulged—empty. So writing a chapter on self-
control seems an impossibility for me because I fail to control
myself time and again. My desires, hopes, dreams, and fanta-
sies control me more than I control them. They speak softly
and seductively: "You will hate it if you don't get that dress.
You need that dress! So get it in all three colors." They tell me
that just one more won't hurt, that to give in this time is okay,
and that nobody is perfect. My desires know all the tricks,
and they are hard to resist because everything they offer is just
what I want. It's like having a marketing team entirely bent on
selling me all the things that I love. What an easy job! All they
have to do is say one thing like, "You deserve this," or, "One
more won't hurt," and I'm diving into the deep end, ready for
the time of my life.

Am I Too Weak for Self-Control?

Fortunately, self-control requires weakness. There must be a natural tendency to sin and to self-promotion in order for self-control to be practiced. It is meant for the human being, not the heavenly being, because self-control is the act of refusing to listen to and obey your flesh with all its passions, lusts, and sinful desires; and God has no such temptations. Self-control is necessary in the life of faith because self-control denies self rather than handing over control to self. Self-control is a fruit of the Spirit, and, as such, it involves an act of surrender, of giving the reigns of one's life over to God himself so that through his Spirit within us, we won't do the very thing our selves really want to do.

Like Paul in Romans 7, we find ourselves continually saying that we are doing what we don't want to do, and what we do, we hate. In situations where we say to ourselves, "Don't do it, don't take that last piece of cake," or, "Don't say it; keep your mouth shut," we can quickly reject all those thoughts and instead open our mouths to sin. And in these moments we easily notice our ugly lack of self-control. But these are just the moments that we notice. How many more times do we turn our lives over to our self-will, firmly rejecting God's will, without even noticing it? How many times do we become so distracted by regret, doubt, bitterness, or discontentment that we give up all self-control and become completely consumed with these emotions and thought patterns, completely abandoning the mindfulness of the Spirit that accompanies abiding in Christ? In these moments, we can be so overwhelmed with self that self-control isn't even in the back of our minds, let alone the front. So loud is the voice of self, so aggressive our self-will, that we pay no attention to the Spirit that whispers quietly within our hearts.

For many years I looked at the list of the fruit of the Spirit and assumed that they were gifts given only in part to certain individuals. Like the gifts of the Spirit you see in 1 Corinthians 12, I assumed that I might get one or two of the fruit in my life and never see the others because, after all, I wasn't perfect. That was how I excused my lack of self-control. "Certainly God meant that only for the gifted, the special, the selected ones who can show the rest of us what God could do," I reasoned. But as we have seen, **the fruit of the Spirit is a natural outpouring of a life turned over to the Spirit of God** and so not reserved for the select few. This truth changes things. It means that self-control no longer has to elude you. It means that if you are in Christ, you can deny yourself and refuse to give in to your passions and whims, and can instead choose to obey God out of your love for him.

What Is Self-Control?

Many might think of self-control as a character trait of strong and confident people who, through dogged determination, do what they want to do, achieve what they want to achieve, and succeed the way they want to succeed. For the people who, through determination and rigorous self-control, manage their lives into the perfection they desire, self-control is everything. When you consider self-control as foundational to all that is good in your life, even to the very fruit we are talking about in this book, you replace the vine that is Christ with self—your determination, will, strength, and righteousness. But this is a severe misunderstanding of self-control as it is described in Galatians 5:23. Self-control isn't the source of all the other fruit. As we have seen, the source is the Holy Spirit himself. So what of self-control? How can that be listed as a fruit of the Spirit when it so clearly seems about self rather than Spirit?

The Ability to Be Self-Controlled

Self-control is the best fruit to end with because **self-control is about subduing self, restraining it**, through the Holy Spirit who lives in us and animates Christ's life in us. This fruit, self-control, helps us cultivate the other fruit. Where peace and gentleness have not yet blossomed in your life, where you have failed to be faithful or kind, self-control can help the process.

When you first start to study the fruit of the Spirit, you can easily be hit with how little you experience them. And then you can become overwhelmed with the degree of 'work' set before you to improve your fruit production. The task seems daunting. But if you will see self-control as continually setting your mind on the things of the Spirit, something amazing will happen. Many areas of besetting sin will become less natural and fruitfulness more supernatural. I once was sorely lacking in areas of joy, peace, patience, gentleness, and more, but since I've started to be more mindful of these fruit, to learn more about them, to meditate on them and to see his hands and his life in them, they have started to appear more and more in my life. The Holy Spirit, through God's Word and the application of it to your life, can and will change your life, and this will bring you more joy, peace, and patience than you ever thought possible.

One time recently after speaking at a women's conference, I was overwhelmed by the number of women who approached me afterward and thanked me for being direct, yet kind and gentle. I was confounded. How did that happen? My passion hadn't lessened. I wasn't less interested in their salvation or healing. Yet my spirit had changed. Kind and gentle is not my nature, but I see evidence of transformation. And I owe this not to my doing, to my hard work or determination, but simply to setting my mind to the things of the Spirit. I am simply now trusting him to do his work in me.

> We might say that self-control is not control by oneself through one's own willpower but rather control of oneself through the Holy Spirit. —Jerry Bridges

Self-Surrender

So we've seen that self-control isn't turning your life over to yourself to control. It isn't the act of governing yourself, of believing in yourself, or even of loving yourself enough to make right choices. Self-control is about surrendering yourself to God so that the Holy Spirit can have his way within you. It is about turning your life over to him fully, to make of it what he will. It's about allowing yourself to be governed not by self, but by God. Practically speaking, it's about self-restraint, holding your self-life back, not giving it control or empowering it to make a change but turning all of your desires onto God, seeking him, knowing him, loving him.

In Mark 8:34 Jesus says, "*If anyone would come after me, let him deny himself and take up his cross and follow me.*" **So self-control begins in self-death.** As long as the self-life is alive and kicking, as long as self is calling the shots and making the decisions, the Spirit is being ignored and the fruit of the Spirit stifled. This is the problem we read about in Romans 8 where it says, "*For those who live according to the flesh set their minds on the things of the flesh*" (v. 5a). The flesh refers to the self-life, the life focused on our dreams, hopes, desires, and feelings. When our thoughts are focused on ourselves, we have set our minds on the things of the flesh, and from this comes the fruit of the flesh. But as we read further in Romans 8, we see that "*those who live according to the Spirit set their minds on the things of the Spirit*" (v. 5b). In this we turn the thoughts of self over to the thoughts of the Spirit. And out of this comes the self-control listed in Galatians 5, this self-control that allows us to submit to God's law and obey it, as we read in

Romans 8:7: "*For the mind that is set on the flesh is hostile to God, for it does not submit to God's law; indeed, it cannot.*" So the mind that is focused on self cannot submit to God's law. Yet how many times do we turn our mind's eye to self, to the desires we have, the feelings, the needs, the strength, the determination, and away from Spirit, from the focus on his Word, his thoughts, and his will?

Self-control, then, is gained only through self-abandonment or self-surrender, the giving up of one's self entirely to the Spirit of God. In this act of surrender we walk away from the competition of life. We reject the world's whispers and pleadings and refuse to withhold ourselves from the God who loves us and would lead and guide us into all righteousness. Certainly nonbelievers can exhibit varying degrees of self-control, but no matter how determined they are, self-control born out of the flesh is of no value in producing the fruit of the Spirit. While unbelievers might control themselves enough to appear to be loving, joyful, kind, patient, and gentle, it will always be only an imitation of the fruit of the Spirit.

Desiring God for More Than Approval

Imitation fruit isn't just an issue for unbelievers. Christian girls might abstain from sex so that they won't get pregnant or get in trouble from their church or family. Some might refrain from overindulging in food because they deeply desire to be thin, or from gossip because they want people to think highly of them. But in all these cases their abstinence is a pure act of the flesh, rather than of the Spirit. Self-control is about desiring God more than approval or attention. And it is out of this deep desire to love God over self that self-control is born. In fact, it is out of this desire for God that faith is born. Once we want God so badly that we turn our very lives over to him, the change begins, and his Holy Spirit works in us to make us new creatures, to change our very nature and transform us into the likeness of his Son.

Self-Restraint

Self-control isn't something you exercise effortlessly but something you must be mindful of in the Spirit daily. If it came natural to man, then it would belong to the body and not to the soul. For example, people who refrain from sexual sin because they are never tempted aren't exercising self-control. That isn't self-control, because it involves no self-restraint. Your strong desires for doing what you don't want to do, the temptation you feel, isn't a sin, but giving in or indulging those desires is sin. Where there is a lack of temptation, there is no need for the fruit of self-control. I personally don't need self-control in the area of drunkenness because I don't like the taste of alcohol. Self-control is exercised in those areas where self is seeking to be satisfied at the expense of God's will. So then, self-control is choosing God over all the impulses to satisfy yourself.

Self-Indulgence or Self-Control?

So we are left with two choices: self-indulgence or self-control. Self-indulgence is the act of giving in, of choosing pleasing self over pleasing God, loving the flesh over loving the Spirit. In these instances we fail to surrender our will, and instead we exert it. But the life lived in the Spirit subdues the flesh as the Spirit reminds us of God's love for us and our love for him over our love for ourselves.

Indulging Your Personality

Many of us use our personalities as an escape clause for self-control. We say things like, "I can't help it; that's just how I am." And in those instances we serve ourselves while we cover our ears to the whispers of the Spirit. But spiritual fruit never grows from natural temperament. It is a part of who you are, but only of who you are in the flesh. The real question is who are you in Christ. As you turn your mind over to the things of the Spirit, and as you begin to feed and nourish the fruit of the Spirit in your life by abandoning yourself to him, your personality will begin to change. And what used to define you will begin to melt away as you become more like Christ and less like man. The personality that serves itself fails to serve God. But the personality that serves God grows fruit in abundance.

You may have an addictive personality. You may have a sullen personality or an aggressive one, but no matter the descriptor you have assigned to yourself, it must not define you or keep you from becoming more like Christ. When you love Christ, this love defines you. His personality becomes your own, and that means change. What you used to see as a natural part of who you are is going to change, because it is inconsistent with who he is, and this is what it means to die to self. When an area of your personality conflicts with his, your love for him compels you to reject your own human nature.

The Indulgence of Comfort

Self-control, then, isn't indulging yourself and your ways, but dying to them. If you are controlled by anything other than God himself, then in the power of the Spirit you must exercise self-control so that you'll become what God intends for you to be. For years I was controlled by comfort. I felt such a need for it, I determined that without it I would not be happy. So I would sin in order to find comfort. And I believe for many of us, comfort is king, ruling over much of our waking lives. Comfort rears its ugly head in hundreds of ways in the life of faith.

For example, **laziness is self-indulgence in the pursuit of comfort.** It is out of serving self that we resist controlling ourselves and doing what God has made the way for us to do. It is self-indulgence, not self-control, that keeps us in bed in the morning, when to rise early and pray is to devote the day to our God.

We comfort ourselves with food when we indulge in more than we need. We comfort ourselves with emotions like bitterness, resentment, revenge, and lust to coddle our flesh. We comfort and serve ourselves with self-pity rather than trusting that whatever God has allowed is for our good. And as we comfort ourselves, we reject self-control in favor of self-indulgence. When we allow ourselves to wallow in excess, in obsession, lust, anger, rage, extravagance, or pleasure-seeking, we reject the fruit of the Spirit in favor of the fruit of the flesh. But all of this can change. Self-control can be yours; it just requires a readjusting of your vision and a desire to look deeply into the things of God so that you might no longer live by your flesh but by his Spirit alone.

> A good many Christians are living a low life — a life of failure and of sin — instead of rest and victory, because they began to say: "I cannot, it is impossible." —Andrew Murray

But How?

If God the Holy Spirit takes up residence in each believer, why is the fruit of that Spirit so lacking in our lives? Why are we not under a constant spell of love, joy, peace, patience, and all the rest? Why are we plagued, instead, with their opposites, and how do we live a life with the Spirit in mind rather than the flesh? **The root of the problem is that we trust ourselves too much.** "But I don't trust myself at all," you say. "I know I am a mess and can't ever seem to get things right." And while that sounds like the truth, the fact is that when we look to ourselves to muster the strength to be good, to be self-controlled, to obey, we are trusting ourselves to do what can only be done in the power of the Spirit. Only through him can we grow in the fruit of the Spirit. It isn't by your own strength and will power that you gain self-control but by turning your mind to the things of God, looking to him, thinking of him, and learning of him. As you redirect your thoughts to the things of the Spirit, self-control, the ability to live out God's Word, is the supernatural outcome.

In his book *Man, the Dwelling Place of God*, A. W. Tozer tells the story of David Brainerd, who once said you can compare "a man without the power of the Spirit trying to do spiritual work to a workman without fingers attempting to do manual labor."[18] Tozer adds to this, saying: "The Holy Spirit is not a luxury meant to make deluxe Christians, as an illuminated frontispiece and a leather binding make a deluxe book. The Spirit is an imperative necessity. Only the Eternal Spirit can do eternal deeds. Millions take for granted that it is possible to live for Christ without first having died with Christ. This is a serious error and we dare not leave it unchallenged."[19]

And this death that he speaks of is your life. This death of Christ with which you identify as a believer is the key to becoming the Fruitful Wife you were meant to be. It was the death of Jesus that purchased your atonement, your justification, and your sanctification, and Romans 6 speaks to this foundational aspect of the Christian life. Our repeated failure to manifest peace in our lives is the effect of our sinful flesh; it is because we sin in reaction to the actions of those around us that we are unfruitful.

But Romans 6 offers all of us freedom from this cycle and a way out of those things we struggle against in marriage. So before we go any further, let's first understand that the death that sets you free from the flesh has already taken place, and here is its reward. Paul asks this same question we are asking:

How can we who died to sin still live in it? Do you not know that all of us who have been baptized into Christ Jesus were baptized into his death? We were buried therefore with him by baptism into death, in order that, just as Christ was raised from the dead by the glory of the Father, we too might walk in newness of life. For if we have been united with him in a death like his, we shall certainly be united with him in a resurrection like his. We know that our old self was crucified with him in order that the body of sin might be brought to nothing, so that we would no longer be enslaved to sin. Now if we have died with Christ, we believe that we will also live with him. We know that Christ, being raised from the dead, will never die again; death no longer has dominion over him. For the death he died he died to sin, once for all, but the life he lives he lives to God. **So you also must consider yourselves dead to sin and alive to God in Christ Jesus.** Let not sin therefore reign in your mortal body, to make you obey its passions. Do not present your members to sin as instruments for unrighteousness, but present yourselves to God as those who have been brought from death to life, and your members to God as instruments for righteousness. **For sin will have no dominion over you, since you are not under law but under grace.** (Rom. 6:2–14)

And there is the key: sin has no dominion over you anymore, which means it is no longer your master; you are no longer its slave, destined to do whatever it would bid you to do. Things that seem to dominate us in relationships—worry, doubt, fear, bitterness, resentment—are powerful emotions that shake the fruit right out of our lives and leave it to rot on the ground around us. But Romans 6 sheds a different light on the idea of struggle. If we will identify our struggles as sins, then we can find our instant freedom from them.

There was a time when all of us were slaves to sin, when we were chained up and bound to commit them. But Jesus came to set us free from sin, not just to spend eternity in heaven but to be free from sin's power over us here on earth. And when he did that, he removed the padlock that held the chains of sin to our hands and feet. But too often we have continued to walk around with the chains still on, forgetting, not being mindful of the fact that the padlock was taken off. And so we struggle with sin rather than allow Christ to be fully done with it for us.

And so the question now is not, how can I muster the strength to be self-controlled, but, when will I lift my hands and allow the chains to fall off and become fully free from the sin that used to control me? Sin is no longer your master, for you are not under law but under grace. And it is this grace that will allow you to see the self-control of the Spirit in your life.

Is Self-Control Possible?

The most important words in the pursuit of self-control are found in Luke 18:27: "*The things which are impossible with men are possible with God.*" In other words, your self-control, an actual impossibility for you, is completely possible with God, because "**nothing will be impossible with God**" (Luke 1:37).

We can no longer use the notion of the impossibility of self-control as an escape from the authentic counsel of God and his Word. To do so is to serve a lie rather than the truth and to continue to rely on self to do what only God himself can do in you. Unfortunately, many of us, having failed to realize this fact, have in sad resignation given ourselves permission to fail before failing. No one is perfect, after all. So, getting in line behind all the imperfect people in the world, we begin to replace self-control with "respectable sin." These sins that we deem to be too dug in, too much a part of the very fiber of our being to be removed, are accepted as immovable objects that are intrinsic to our nature. To remove them would be to change our very being, the core of who we are. We therefore, make exceptions for these "small" sins in our lives, and we give ourselves permission to sin. And in these moments we choose self-indulgence over self-control.

Is a Lack of Self-Control Respectable?

These respectable sins, as Jerry Bridges calls them in his book by the same name, include a lack of self-control. When you give yourself permission to be out of control, you endorse a sin that much of the church has turned a blind eye to, considering it too impossible or even too out of date. And so we look upon the words we read in 1 Timothy 2:9, words that describe how godly women ought to adorn themselves, words like, "*with modesty and self-control*," and we take a pass, we play the grace card, and we reject the effort that we believe such obedience would take. And then we come to 1 Timothy 5:6 and wonder, is it true? Is "*she who is self-indulgent . . . dead even while she lives?*"

We must never, through our resistance to the idea of self-control, make our confession a pillow for sin. We are all, as Paul says, "wretched" and in need of salvation. But thank God that "*there is therefore now no condemnation for those who are in Christ Jesus*" (Rom. 8:1). I say all of this so that you can see with your eyes the danger of a lack of self-control and how easy it is to accept it. But we can't stop the conversation there. It must be affirmed that our lack of self-control isn't grounds for condemnation but for confession. And once confession has been made, then change starts to take place.

Why Do We Need Self-Control?

Self-control is necessary in the life of faith. If we can't control ourselves—in other words, subdue our flesh—then we are no longer controlled by our love for God. The very nature of love is to please the loved one, and the believer should love no one more than God. Therefore, self-control as the product of this love, as the fruit of the Spirit of love, is a supernatural part of the believing life. Not that we are sin free, 100 percent self-controlled, but the life lived in love with God and in pursuit of his thoughts defaults to self-abandon, and therefore to self-control rather than being controlled by the flesh.

Growing the fruit of self-control is instrumental in maintaining all the other fruit, and is often a complementary step in the process. But self-control born out of duty or obligation withers quickly.

CONCLUSION

CONCLUSION
Growing Abundant Fruit

Let me end this work by talking about how the fruit grows—what we do and what the Spirit does.

In the life of faith there is a continual tension between work and fruit, an uncertainty of the degree of participation of man and of God. In the quest to fully grasp how the fruit of the Spirit is produced in us, consider that **a machine can do work, but only the presence of life can grow fruit.**

Work refers to effort, to labor, but the amazing thing about fruit is that it is the supernatural product of the vine. The branch doesn't labor and struggle independently of the vine to produce fruit; it simply remains attached to the vine, and as the sap of life flows through the vine, so it flows through the branch. In John 15:4 Jesus puts it to us this way: *"Abide in me, and I in you. As the branch cannot bear fruit by itself, unless it abides in the vine, neither can you, unless you abide in me."* Even though a farmer works hard at tending his crops, he can't do anything to create the fruit. Only the vine has in it what is necessary for life. And so it is for us. It is because of the vine that we can grow any fruit at all. So then, why was all the paper wasted in printing this book, if it all rests on the vine? Because there exists for man a role to play, and that isn't a passive role whereby we sit quietly by as God changes us without our participation. It is an active role that begins as we turn our thoughts toward the vine. This setting of your mind on the Spirit isn't something you do only once; it is something that must continually be done. Each time that our minds wander into areas of the flesh, into areas of darkness, they need to be redirected and brought back to the light. And in the light they will find just what they need for nurturing the fruit the way the farmer does as he waters and cares for his crops.

A. W. Tozer once said, "True faith is not passive but active. It requires that we meet certain conditions, that we allow the teachings of Christ to dominate our total lives from the moment we believe. The man of saving faith must be willing to be different from others. The effort to enjoy the benefits of redemption while enmeshed in the world is futile. We must choose one or the other; and faith quickly makes its choice, one from which there is no retreat."[20]

And it is in this spirit that this book was written. The fruit of the Spirit is not generated by man, but man plays an active part in its production as he looks into the Word of God and allows the teachings of Christ to dominate his life. A life of active surrender. A life of active abiding.

Admit You Have a Problem

So before we draw our discussion to a close, let's take a good look at what a mind set on the Spirit looks like. Let's consider some of the things we can do as followers in order to encourage the growth of the fruit in our own lives. The first thing we have to do is the first thing we all must do in order to begin the journey of faith: we must admit that we have a problem. *"Wretched man that I am! Who will deliver me from this body of death?"* (Rom. 7:24). Like Paul, we must see our own wretchedness in the failure to love God and to nurture and grow the fruit of the Spirit in our lives. And we must admit that we are helpless to do anything about it, and with Paul, we must thank God for our Savior: *"Thanks be to God through Jesus Christ our Lord! So then, I myself serve the law of God with my mind, but with my flesh I serve the law of sin"* (Rom. 7:25). The life of faith takes a sober recognition of our own wretchedness.

Once confession is made, once we allow godly sorrow generated by our own failure to work itself out into repentance (2 Cor. 7:10), we must then commit to love God, for it's from that love that we are obedient (John 15:10). In those areas where you have failed to live in the fruit of the Spirit, you must agree with God and commit to obedience where there once was rebellion. There are some who would say that man makes no ground in this attempt to refocus his life onto the fruit produced by the vine, but until there is a moving of the thoughts from the things of the flesh to the things of the Spirit, there is failure.

Tozer refers to this as a will issue when he says, "First of all we must will, for the will is master of the heart."[21] It is the will that must change its commitment from self-indulgence and sin to self-control and obedience. And in order for the will to be exercised in this way, it must get its direction from the Holy Spirit himself, who speaks to the heart of man through the Word of God. As you look into God's Word and are transformed in the process, your will becomes more and more inclined to relinquish its insistence on self-sufficiency and self-indulgence, and fruit will grow.

Surrender

This change in focus and fruit requires an important thing in the life of the believer, and that is not only obedience but also surrender. When it comes to increasing the fruit in your life you must, in all instances, surrender yourself to the will of the Father. As long as there is anything in you that thinks that you can do it in your own strength, as long as you consider it a job for your will or your effort, you will fail to produce any real fruit.

Adore His Omnipotence

You will not trust God's transforming power unless you are certain of his power. In the pursuit of a changed life, the fruitful woman must start with the foundation of God's omnipotence. When you can **adore his power, trust his strength and his perfect might,** then you can accept that he is sufficient for all the change your life requires. Each morning I think about his omnipotence. I adore him for it, and I trust him for it. Where we are certain that God is almighty, we can be certain that we can do all things through him who strengthens us. So as we pursue a life of fruit, we must believe in an omnipotent God.

Die to Self

As Jesus says in John 12:24, *"Unless a grain of wheat falls into the earth and dies, it remains alone; but if it dies, it bears much fruit."* So it is with us. **In order for there to be much fruit there must be much death.** So it is important in any discussion of spiritual growth to understand the self-death that we all must face before any real change can be made. We die to self by rejecting our flesh with all its passions and desires, and we walk instead in the way of the Spirit. Romans 13:14 warns us to *"make no provision for the flesh, to gratify its desires."* The provisions that we make keep the flesh as a counselor, as an active voice in our choices and thoughts. But to continue to allow the flesh a voice in our life is to subdue the voice of the Spirit and to reject his will as secondary to our own. In order for the fruit of the Spirit to grow in a life, that life must first be put to death, a death that denies everything that the life has held dear in favor of everything that God holds dear.

Discipline Yourself

To discipline yourself is to control yourself; it is to not allow your flesh to have mastery over you. This can sound like a harsh statement in a world bent on self-indulgence at any cost, but in order to turn our minds away from the flesh, we have to take the opportunity to say no to its promptings. When speaking on a lack of self-control, Bridges relates the story of his love for ice cream and his desire for mastery over his flesh. He says:

> I think of my own craving for ice cream years ago when I would have a dish of it at dinner and another at bedtime. In that situation God convicted me of my lack of self-control by causing me to see that a seemingly benign practice greatly weakened my self-control in other more critical areas. I learned that we cannot pick and choose the areas in life where we will exercise self-control.[22]

He goes on to tell the story of walking past an ice cream shop, and though he wasn't in the habit of overindulging any longer, he still denied himself a dish because, as he says, "I needed to say 'no' to myself just for the purpose of keeping that desire under control."[23] This idea of saying no to ourselves in order to train ourselves in self-control is a fantastic one. If you lack self-control in one area, don't underestimate the value of exerting self-control in other areas. The more accustomed you get to resisting your flesh, the more room you leave for the Spirit, and so the more room for abundant fruit.

> Do you not know that in a race all the runners run, but only one receives the prize? So run that you may obtain it. Every athlete exercises self-control in all things. They do it to receive a perishable wreath, but we an imperishable. So I do not run aimlessly; I do not box as one beating the air. But I discipline my body and keep it under control, lest after preaching to others I myself should be disqualified.
> —1 Corinthians 9:24–27

Focus on the Truth

As you determine to change your focus from the flesh to the Spirit, the most important thing to remember is this: *"Whatever is true, whatever is honorable, whatever is just, whatever is pure, whatever is lovely, whatever is commend-*

able, if there is any excellence, if there is anything worthy of praise, think about these things" (Phil. 4:8). **The fruit of the Spirit is given the freedom to grow in a life that accepts only what is true and honorable to be its every thought.** When we allow lies to become our truth, then the fruit of the Spirit is dashed from our lives. And it is not a rare thing to believe a lie, and even to perpetuate it. As you struggle with the sins in your life, it is essential that you allow the Word of God to shine the light on them all. We can no longer, as women of God, allow the lies of the world to be our yardstick of acceptability.

The truth is that every problem in your life has sin as its root. It may not be your sin, but somewhere at the bottom of it there is sin, and the prescription for the sin that seems to have mastery over us is found in the life of Christ and what he has already done. In every case, addressing our own sinful reactions, thoughts, feelings, and actions; confessing them as sin; and repenting from them bring onto us the glorious grace of God, and with that the freedom of forgiveness. And then we are able to move forward in the knowledge that though we are not perfect, we are his, and if we are his, then we have living within us all that we need for every fruit listed in Galatians 5:22–23.

When the fruit of the Spirit seems far from us, we must continue to search for truth found in God's Word and apply it to our failure. In Paul's words the thought goes like this: *"I do not consider that I have made it my own. But one thing I do: forgetting what lies behind and straining forward to what lies ahead"* (Phil. 3:13). To allow discouragement to replace hope is to believe a lie. You fail; no surprise there. We are all sinful, and so we must fail, but we must not allow our failure to convince us of lies and to distract us from the Father. But in all things consider the truth: *"Not by might, nor by power, but by my Spirit, says the LORD of hosts"* (Zech. 4:6). You must remember always and say to yourself that *"I can do all things through him who strengthens me"* (Phil. 4:13). When it comes to suffering, to trials, to obedience in all things, it is Christ who strengthens you and makes the fruit abundant in your life.

Put on the Spiritual Armor

In the lives of us all, there will be battles, challenges, failures, and setbacks, but God has made a way for his children. And he has given us protection in the form of the spiritual armor. If you haven't been in the habit of putting on your spiritual armor on a daily basis, then you are in for a surprise when you do. This isn't just a metaphor but an important practice in the life of faith. As you desire more of the Holy Spirit in your life, as you want more fruit in your daily walk, you must be prepared to start each day off by mentally putting on the spiritual armor found in Ephesians 6:10–18. Especially in the area of self-control, in those areas where the edges are still rough and the fruit hasn't yet fully formed, the spiritual armor is of great importance. **If you want to change your family tree, if you want the fruit that grows from your life and the life of those you love to be spiritual fruit, then begin the habit of practicing putting on your spiritual armor daily.**

Watch for Him

I am a born rule follower. I like rules; they give me parameters, guides, boundaries. And so for years I religiously followed the rule of setting aside devotional time each day with God. I did it as much out of obligation as love. But as my sense of love started to overwhelm my sense of duty, I reminded myself that I am not saved by my depth of devotion, and that my quiet time wasn't meant to improve my life but to glorify him; then things started to change. I found myself each morning looking at the clock in the dark of the early morning, believing that God had woken me up just to spend time with him. And so for the last ten years I have woken without an alarm clock to the gentle tap of the Father on my heart. Every day it's different, but when awake in the early morning with the clock reading 5:00, 4:00, or even 3:00, I get out of bed excited to meet with him and see what he has for me that day.

The fruit of the Spirit flourishes in these moments, in these sweet encounters with the Savior who loved us enough to give his very life for us. When we wake to the memory of his sacrifice, when we are aware of his deep love for us and his desire to meet with us, the morning becomes a fertile and joyful time. The effect of this kind of devotion, not to a schedule but to a relationship, is a renewed spiritual as well as physical energy. And any discussion of the fruit of the Spirit would be incomplete without it.

But maybe God has not taken to waking you up in the dark hours of the morning; perhaps your schedule is too hectic. But should he begin to quietly wake you from your slumber, take a moment to consider what an amazing thing this is, that the Almighty God would come to you and ask you to rise and meet him. Should we all accept this call, how glorious would our fruit become!

Flesh and blood may be the author of this: one man may give another an affecting view of divine things with but common assistance: but God alone can give a spiritual discovery of them. —Jonathan Edwards

It All Comes Back to Love

God wants fruit to be a part of all of his children's lives. He wants abundance in your life, and he can provide it; you need only to begin to become mindful of who he is and how much he has shown his love for you. Set your thoughts not on your flesh with all its lusts but on the Spirit, who is with you. Don't fear if you haven't experienced much fruit in your life. **Being mindful of who God is and his love for you, becoming intimately acquainted with what pleases him, will be like fertilizer to your soul.**

The Holy Spirit lives in you the moment you begin to call Jesus "Lord," and from that the fruit of the Spirit manifests itself increasingly in your life. To expect that it's something that you are able to generate yourself is folly. "*Are you so foolish? Having begun by the Spirit, are you now being perfected by the flesh?*" (Gal. 3:3) Certainly not, but you know that your growth comes from him. You are called to "*walk by the Spirit, [so that] you will not gratify the desires of the flesh. For the desires of the flesh are against the Spirit, and the desires of the Spirit are against the flesh, for these are opposed to each other, to keep you from doing the things you want to do*" (Gal. 5:16–17).

As you abide in the vine, as you find yourself loving the God of the universe, you will naturally become more interested in and aware of your spiritual growth. If you want more of Christ, more perfection, more peace, love, and joy, more fruit, then join me today in devoting your life to the vine. Try it and see if you don't become more fruitful the more you love and worship at his feet. An abundance of fruity goodness can be yours when you turn your life over, with all its passions and lusts, to the Giver of fruit. And while this fruit will bring glory to God by nourishing those around you, it will also serve your soul as it blesses you with a taste of the Father's goodness and the gift of a life lived solely for him.

NOTES

1. George Washington Bethune, *The Fruit of the Spirit* (1845).
2. John Piper, "The Greatest of These Is Love: An Introduction to the Series," Desiring God, http://www.desiringgod.org/resource-library/sermons/the-greatest-of-these-is-love-an-introduction-to-the-series.
3. Corrie ten Boom, *The Hiding Place*, new ed. (London: Hodder & Stoughton, 1976), 172.
4. Megan Grober, "Elisabeth Elliot and Rachel Saint," History Makers, http://www.historymakers.info/inspirational-christians/elisabeth-elliot-a-rachel-saint.html.
5. A. W. Tozer, *The Pursuit of God*, Project Gutenberg e-book (2008), http://www.gutenberg.org/files/25141/25141-h/25141-h.htm.
6. *Merriam-Webster's Collegiate Dictionary*, 10th ed., s.v. "obsession."
7. For more on this topic see Michael and Hayley DiMarco, *Die Young: Burying Your Self in Christ* (Wheaton, IL: Crossway, 2012).
8. Corrie ten Boom, *Tramp for the Lord* (New York: Inspirational, 1995), 106.
9. D. A. Carson, "1 John 5:1–5," in *New Bible Commentary: 21st Century Edition* (Downers Grove, IL: InterVarsity, 1994), emphasis original.
10. Oswald Chambers, *My Utmost for His Highest: Selections for the Year* (Grand Rapids, MI: Discovery, 1993), Jan. 28 entry.
11. Andrew Murray, *The Master's Indwelling* (2004), Project Gutenberg e-book, http://www.gutenberg.org/files/12854/12854-h/12854-h.htm.
12. Robert J. Morgan, *On This Day: 365 Amazing and Inspiring Stories about Saints, Martyrs, and Heroes*, electronic ed. (Nashville: Thomas Nelson, 2000).
13. *Nelson's New Illustrated Bible Dictionary,* ed. Ronald F. Youngblood, F. F. Bruce, et al. (Nashville: Thomas Nelson, 1995).
14. W. E. Vine, Merrill F. Unger et al., *Vine's Complete Expository Dictionary of Old and New Testament Words* (Nashville: Thomas Nelson, 1996).
15. Walter A. Elwell and Philip Wesley Comfort, *Tyndale Bible Dictionary* (Wheaton, IL: Tyndale, 2001).
16. Chambers, *My Utmost for His Highest,* Feb. 23 entry.
17. John Bunyan, *Pilgrim's Progress* (1678).
18. A. W. Tozer, *Man, the Dwelling Place of God* (repr. Camp Hill, PA: WingSpread, 2008), n.p.
19. Ibid.
20. Ibid.
21. Ibid.
22. Jerry Bridges, *Respectable Sins* (Colorado Springs: NavPress, 2007), 110.
23. Ibid.

A CHALLENGE

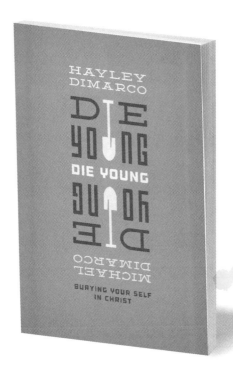

"People bury themselves in things they hope will save them, but the only one who can truly be saved is the one who is buried in Christ. That is the gospel—the saving truth that Christ's love was so compelling, so complete that he would give his own life for yours that you might have eternal life with him."

—Hayley and Michael DiMarco in *Die Young*

"...he died for all, that those who live might no longer live for themselves but for him who for their sake died and was raised."

2 Corinthians 5:15